(10) (11) (12) (10) (11) (12) (13)

Sir   Jerusalem

(1)   statement by woman

5 : 3

worship the Father   worship the Father | worship the Father

(13) (14) (15) (16) (17) | (18) (19) (20)

8 : 5

worship the Father | worship the Father

3 : 2

re: worship   re: Messias

(10) (11) (12) (13) (14) (15) (16) (17) | (18) (19) (20) (13) (21)

Sir, I perceive ... thou art etc.

21:13

3 by woman : 5 by Jesus

I..... am he

(10) 2-idea "octave"

(21)

9

hus-bands   hus-band

(10) (11) (12) (10) (11) (12) (13) (14) (15) (16) (17) (18) (19) (20) (13) (21)

19   20   21   22   23   24   25   26   27   28   29   30   31   32   33   34

Ye worship ye know not what.

FORM:

THE SILENT LANGUAGE

103. MELANCOLIA. 1514. Copperplate engraving.

See page 34.

FORM

THE SILENT LANGUAGE

By
HUGO NORDEN, MUS. DOC.
Professor of Music Theory
Boston University

BOSTON
BRANDEN PRESS
PUBLISHERS

FORM:

THE SILENT LANGUAGE

CONTENTS

PART THE FIRST
Some observations into an immortal conversation

PART THE SECOND
About a fable by Aesop

PROLOGUE

Dynamic Symmetry is a creative force that changes people; and those who permit themselves to be affected by it will never be quite the same again. They will say with Walt Whitman

All truths wait in all things,

. . . .

The insignificant is as big to me as any.

The creative artist—whatever his medium—will find not only a new kind of idea springing into bloom, but he will see his ideas crystallizing themselves into forms of exquisite beauty and impeccable perfection once he becomes aware of Dynamic Symmetry.

But, something else will happen to the creative thinker within whom Dynamic Symmetry has taken hold. He will know when he is right; he will be sure of it, and nothing can dissuade him. He will have the ability and self-confidence to know his position as Leonardo da Vinci knew his when he wrote in the Proem to his celebrated Notebooks:

Many will believe that they can with reason censure me, alleging that my proofs are contrary to the authority of certain men who are held in great reverence by their inexperienced judgements, not taking into account that my conclusions were arrived at as a result of simple and plain experience, which is the true mistress.

These rules enable you to discern the true from the false, and thus to set before yourselves only things possible and of moderation; and they forbid you to use a cloak of ignorance, which will bring about that you attain to no result and in despair abandon yourself to melancholy.

Although the great and eminent Leonardo does not mention Dynamic Symmetry in so many words, several phrases in the above quotation will leap up and strike a responsive chord in many people.

9

How many teachers of composition—either literary or musical—as of this moment can recall students whose efforts "attain to no result and in despair abandon" themselves not only to melancholy but to frustration and defeat? How many instructors of musical instruments will not admit in their candid moments that even some of their most promising pupils bow, finger, blow or pedal under a "cloak of ignorance" and do not actually know what they are doing or why they are doing it? How many students in the creative arts honestly feel that they have the insight or are being given the means whereby they can positively "discern the true from the false"?

And, if we are really honest with ourselves, how often are we not disappointed by the books and lectures of "certain men who are held in great reverence" when we discover that our most conscientious study of their words has not materially improved our products?

There comes a point in the life of every student at which he feels there must be a level of knowledge that is not being made available to him. For instance, in the study of Harmony the 371 Chorales by Johann Sebastian Bach invariably serve as models for the student. These chorales are assigned for so-called "analysis" and in due time the student is given similar chorales to harmonize himself. So, harmonize them he does; and, he and his teacher will certainly see to it that no mistake exists. They are—according to the textbook—absolutely correct; but, they are apt to sound nothing whatever like the flowing and majestic harmonizations by Bach.

What went wrong? Why do these perfectly correct harmonizations sound so innocuous while those of Bach—sometimes less perfect theoretically—are so overpoweringly magnificent? And, what is still more perplexing is the fact that sometimes even the teacher seems unable to put his finger on the trouble! "Oh well, Bach was a genius."

On the other hand, while Bach was unquestionably a genius of the first water, anybody skilled in Dynamic Symmetry and its application to Harmony will comprehend within minutes

10

exactly what sort of thing happens in the 2265 lines in the Bach Chorale harmonizations, and it will be readily seen that this is not ordinarily taught in the usual academic procedures. From there on, it is not difficult for any student with ordinary intelligence to harmonize any melody artistically as well as correctly.

Or, in another field: what magic does the instructor of an instrument possess when with a few slight changes of fingering, perhaps, he transforms a cumbersome passage into a smoothly flowing one? Or, what secret skill does the concert artist employ when he makes a piece sound entirely different from the best performance that a student can produce, even though the student can play as rapidly and, externally at least, on a level well comparable with that of the artist? In other words what makes one player "tick" while another seems to make no contact communicatively or emotionally with his audience?

While to a large extent factors of personality and taste do enter into these situations, the objective listener will soon see that much of the success of a virtuoso performance is due to Dynamic Symmetry, applied—perhaps by sheer instinct—by the executants.

As Walt Whitman put it, "All truths wait in all things," and once one becomes aware of Dynamic Symmetry he will see that this too waits in all good and well-wrought things. In fact, the commonplace things that have surrounded him all his life suddenly take on an entirely fresh significance.

An Aesop fable or the Beatitudes or the 23rd Psalm blossom forth as truly wonderful formal structures. A Catholic all at once sees in the arrangement of the fourteen Stations of the Cross a multiplicity of interlocking symbolic ratios. A Bach Invention is transformed from a dreary finger exercise to a complex form of incredible perfection and ingenuity.

Dynamic Symmetry, for the most part, is not in our day widely recognized and accepted as a basis for creative thinking, although copious evidence of its application exists in the works of virtually every successful artist in every medium. Thus, a basis for formal organization that has been in successful use

11

by the foremost artists and writers for thousands of years is now almost entirely overlooked in academic artistic circles. In fact, not only is it overlooked, but most creative artists today know almost nothing about it. And, because so little is known about Dynamic Symmetry, many students and teachers—when told about it for the first time—tend to reject it.

Although the mainstream of academic thought in the arts today takes little or no cognizance of Dynamic Symmetry and goes its way without it and in many cases with quite dubious results, a few writers and teachers recognize its value and make it known. However, they meet with an ever-present obstacle: in our day many people find it repulsive to think of art, religion, or music, as an expression of serious systematic thought; and most students rebel mightily against being required to plan out in detail a projected composition.

What eludes these students is that Dynamic Symmetry, quite the opposite from being a restraining force to deter their creative faculties from free expression, proves to be a means for channeling their inmost feelings and personality into their compositions. And, when all of the musical techniques, such as Harmony, Counterpoint, Canon, Fugue, etc., are seen and understood in the light of Dynamic Symmetry these sciences also become channels whereby the composer can literally enter and live within his works. Similar applications occur in the practice of the other arts. But, when taken in the ordinary academic manner with no awareness of Dynamic Symmetry, these branches of the musical knowledge are nothing but the sterile and fruitless "disciplines" that most students and even some teachers believe them to be.

The writing of this book presented a problem from the very beginning. The temptation was to make it much larger and develop in into a full-scale treatise on the place of Dynamic Symmetry in the creative arts. But, this, on second thought, would have been a wearisome task for both author and reader. And when books become wearying they lose their impact. Thus, it was decided to say just enough to let some serious students know that an underlying force exists that they can bring into play in their works if they so desire. Some—perhaps many—will find no place in their thinking for what follows and will reject it. But, for those whose minds are open to the exciting possibility of aligning themselves with a creative principle of unlimited potentiality, this little volume is written and it is hoped that thereby a door will open for them to explore a new path of creativity and that it will lead to many exhilirating surprises.

It works! As the revered Leonardo da Vinci so aptly put it; "simple and plain experience" tells the tale.

PART THE FIRST

Some observations into an immortal conversation

CHAPTER I

"...maintenance involves perpetual creation, as permanence involves a perpetual springing forth." So writes one of the most significant scientists and thinkers of the 18th century.

Thus every moment that we live and in everybody and everything that we see about us, something of the creative process is in operation. We cannot escape it; nor can the creative process by-pass us—in fact, not for a single moment.

Large organizations, as is the case with individuals, are constantly exercising the creative process in order to maintain or improve their position. Industrial concerns introduce new products or make old ones more attractive. Nations propose and exercise new programs to benefit and appeal to the people. Churches, clubs and lodges devise new means and intensify time-tested ones to attract new followers as well as to satisfy their faithful members. Entertainers develop new performance routines, and concert performers improve their techniques and extend their repertoires. Educators ever strive for more effective methods and try to increase the functionality of their courses. Composers and painters develop new techniques and put old means of expression to new uses. Theologians bend every effort to make doctrines and beliefs applicable to contemporary living. Novelists, playwrights and poets labor in the cause of greater realism in keeping with life and attitudes of today.

All this is "perpetual creation" in motion!

But, what is this all-pervading creative process? How can one crystallize it into practical terms? And, how can it be put into effective and gratifying use?

In essence the creative process is application of the principle of Division in the sense of separation. And, the division sign and the fraction line—both of which do the same thing—are without a doubt the most universally productive of all symbols.

The great and awesome importance of division as the creative

17

process was understood even in the earliest times. Within the first eighteen verses of the first chapter of Genesis, the verb "divide" occurs *five* times—*twice* in the past tense and *three* times in the present. And in the second chapter of the same book we read that "a river went out of Eden" and "was parted" (that is, divided) to bring into being four valuable and productive land areas.

Of the almost numberless tales of creative division related in the Bible an especially dramatic one is given in the sixteenth chapter of Numbers. A frightful plague was killing the children of Israel at a staggering rate whereupon Aaron—upon instructions from Moses—"stood between the dead and the living; and the plague was stayed." In other words, the division of the remaining healthy people from the contaminated ones brought order out of utter chaos.

And in one of his most powerful utterances, Jesus said, "Suppose ye that I am come to give peace on earth? I tell you, Nay; but rather division: For from henceforth there shall be *five* in one house divided, *three* against *two* and *two* against *three*."[1]

Our whole system of living is based upon the fact that somebody back in remotest antiquity hit upon the idea of dividing time into units that can be measured, grouped and subsequently apportioned to our daily requirements. The commuter who catches the 5:15 local, the young couple who meet for an 8 o'clock "date," the child who must come in from his play at 4:30, the worshippers who flock to church at 11 on Sunday and the prisoner counting the days until his release all have one thing in common. They are every one partaking in activities and situations made possible by the systematic division of time into units that can be further subdivided. And this division and subdivision proceeds downwards from centuries to decades, from decades to years, from years to months, from months to weeks and so on through days, hours, minutes and seconds. Yes, and athletes sometimes compete even to fractions of a second. Herein lies one of the

1) Luke, Chapter 12, v. 51, 52.

most important aspects of form; namely, that even the smallest component part of a form must be as perfect as is the form itself. A person with a relatively slight deformity, such as a defective arm, is considered disabled to some degree. Likewise, a musical composition, building, poem or painting which has a defect in the smallest and seemingly insignificant parts of its form, must be considered imperfect.

The very table on which this book was lying before you began to read it is the result of division. Had some skilled craftsman not divided the wood from which it was made according to some pre-arranged plan, there still would be only the rough logs and *no* table from which to pick up a book.

When musicians play a chord they divide the octave vertically according to mathematical proportions specified by the composer as made avilable by nature itself through the harmonic series. Without such a division of the octave into acoustically correct proportions there would be no harmony or counterpoint, merely an indefinable mass of unintelligible sound. And when the separate notes of the chord are played by the musicians, each man must divide his string length or wind column into the proportions specified by the notation indicating the composer's designs.

But, this is not the musician's only division problem. At the same time that he is busy dividing the octave vertically, he is also dividing a pre-established time span into rhythms, phrases, themes, sections and movements. This, too, is according to the composer's mathematical calculations—whether these are conscious or instinctive. The painter, likewise, achieves form by dividing the area of his canvas into orderly segments by means of lines, color, figures, light and shadows.

And, in the last analysis, architecture—which has been poetically described as "frozen music"—is nothing but a segment of space divided from the much larger space around it. This "captured" segment of space is then subdivided into lesser spaces designed to meet specific requirements. Your kitchen, living room, church, concert hall, prison, hospital and corner drug store are all such segments of space made possible by the architect's skill in subduing the laws of gravity to the extent that he succeeded in dividing these spaces from the vast space around them.

Once a person becomes aware of division as an act of creativity he is changed. He can never be the same again. Every phase of his life is changed. His time has to be divided between work, recreation, sleep, helping those in need, worshipping, praying, etc. He is expected to divide his substance between living expenses, charity, taxes and whatever obligations come his way. Even the food he eats is divided into proper proportions of various kinds. All these divisions make for successful and pleasant living, and each act of division in whatever form it may appear is a partaking of the great creative principle—whether it be giving of time, spending of money or eating dinner.

With this awareness that one's living is part of an all—encompassing law, how can a person ever again be indolent, careless or wasteful? As usual, the Bible says it better, "Render to Caesar the things that are Caesar's, and to God the things that are God's."[2]

This, however, hints at the possibility of faulty division, and in three Gospels we read that "a house divided against itself" can come to destruction. So an artist or composer who permits faulty division of time or texture to mar his production can anticipate failure and frustration.

Our civil, moral and religious codes have strong words and deterrent measures against those who divide their money, time and affections in ways that are detrimental to themselves and others. In fact, what else is a crime, sin, debt or infidelity but a demonstration of an improper and imprudent division of time, money, energy or affection?

Look about you; think, and partake of this universal and never-ending excitement. Everything you hear, see, taste, smell, touch, feel, hate or think is the result of division. Without division nothing has form and without form nothing exists.

Thus, Division is the first facet of Form: The Silent Language.

2) Mark, Chapter 12 v. 17.

CHAPTER II

The great divisive principle that has influenced the techniques of the world's foremost artists, writers and craftsmen throughout the ages is that commonly known as Dynamic Symmetry. Dr. Glenn Clark in his little book entitled *God's Reach* calls it "the secret of the ages" in an outburst of enthusiasm.

The principle can be stated thus:

In dividing any distance, quantity, area or time span into two parts, the smaller part is to the greater as the greater part is to the whole.

Mathematically, two parts of a whole related to each other in terms of Dynamic Symmetry will bear the ratio of $1 : 1.618$. This exact ratio, however, is a theoretical norm that cannot often be accurately translated into usable practical numbers.

In the early 13th century the Italian mathematician Leonardo Fibonacci, also known as Leonardo of Pisa, became interested in Arabian mathematics and as a result translated this ratio into a summation series that gives this principle in terms of rough proportions:

$1 : 2 : 3 : 5 : 8 : 13 : 21 : 34 : 55 : 89 : 144$, etc.

In practical application any three adjacent numbers of this series can operate in the following way. Take, for example, a whole consisting of 13 aliquot parts which can be expressed fractionally as $\frac{13}{13}$. Divided on the basis of Dynamic Symmetry, this would be separated into two basic and interrelated units of $\frac{5}{13}$ and $\frac{8}{13}$.

Of course, 5 to 8 does not quite show the ratio of 1 : 1.618, neither does 8 to 13. Actually, 5 to 8 is a little under (1.6) and 8 to 13 is a bit too high (1.625). But as will be seen in future chapters, this slight theoretical discrepancy is of no real importance in the exercising of the creative process.

The series shown above becomes more telling when it is preceded by an introductory 1:

1 : 1 : 2 : 3 : 5 : 8 etc.

It would, perhaps, be even clearer if the two ones were written fractionally:

$\frac{1}{1}$: 2 : 3 : 5 : 8 etc.

But, with the two ones, a new series comes into being that is less generally understood and is only infrequently seen in operation. By adding every other number the parallel or secondary series comes about as follows:

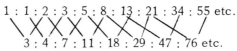

This is known as the Lucas Series.

The proximity of this derivative series to the theoretical norm does not become apparent until the higher figures are considered. For instance, 18 and 29 have the ratio of 1.611, and 29 and 47 that of 1.621.

The relationship of these two series is seen more clearly when the process of adding every other number of the second, or Lucas, series is repeated. The result will be the first series multiplied by 5.

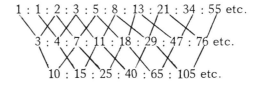

This last series could be espressed very simply in the following terms:

$$2 \times 5 : \underline{3} \times 5 : \underline{5} \times 5 : \underline{8} \times 5 : \underline{13} \times 5 : \underline{21} \times 5 \text{ etc.}$$

But, this is not a mathematical treatise. Neither is it a textbook on form. It is merely intended to give a few clues to establish a norm and a trend of thought to composers, artists, writers and anybody interested in creative living. To this end, we shall limit ourselves to dissecting one well-known passage from St. John's Gospel—the conversation between Jesus and the Woman of Samaria beside Jacob's well in the little city of Sychar.

If we could put into our first chapter that "the Bible *says* it better", we can well afford to say here that "the Bible *does* it better" when it comes to illustrating and defining forms. But just as Johann Sebastian Bach's *The Art of the Fugue* demonstrated the intricacies and artistic possibilities of fugal composition, so the Bible demonstrates form through an incredible number and variety of models. But, neither *The Art of the Fugue* nor the Bible include a word of explanation as to the structure or communicative purpose of these forms. And, curiously enough, both books illustrate—insofar as form goes—essentially the same thing.

In *The Art of the Fugue* Bach makes his demonstrations by means of tightly organized fugal compostions, whereas the Bible does it through the distribution of ideas in significant passages. And, since ideas are the mainstay and substance of every artistic or literary endeavor in whatever realm, it is immaterial whether the ideas come in the form of verbal statements in literature; melodies, rhythms or sonorities in music; figures and colors in painting, or as rooms in a building. Or, in fact, in the apportioning of time, resources and affections in daily living.

While the last thing the Bible does is to classify itself as a book of form models, it gives many clues. The very first one is the repeated use of the verb "divide" in the first chapter of Genesis. And its repetition, it will be recalled from our first

23

chapter, was distributed through a Dynamic Symmetry ratio into *two* in the past tense and *three* in the present tense.

A stronger suggestion is given in Psalm 1. Here we find a thirteen-idea literary structure divided according to the 5 : 8 ratio in retrograde; the first *eight* ideas telling about the righteous man and the closing *five* dealing with the tragic state of the ungodly. The first *eight* ideas are likewise divided into *five* concerning the righteous man's attributes and habits and *three* giving the fruits of his righteousness. Thus, the fifth and eighth statements are important as the terminal ideas of two formal sections concerning the righteous man.

The fifth idea states about the righteous man that ''in his law doth he meditate day and night.'' The older version in the *Book of Common Prayer* makes it even more emphatic by saying that he will ''exercise himself'' in the law of the Lord day and night. Then, in the eighth idea we read to our amazement that ''whatsoever he doeth shall prosper.''

And in Psalm 119, which consists of a collection of twenty-two multiple forms of the utmost complexity (one for each letter of the Hebrew alphabet), we find the petition, ''open thou mine eyes, that I may behold wondrous things out of thy law.''

It would indeed be arrogant and presumptuous for anybody to say, or even suggest, that ''the law of the Lord'' can be embodied in a mathematical ratio. But, there is much both in the Scriptures and in nature to suggest that Dynamic Symmetry represents at least one aspect of this ''law'' that is accessible to man for study and demonstration. For instance, in addition to the many form demonstrations given in the Bible, we are told that ''God created man in his own image''. One need not consult books to learn that this ''image'' of God is built according to the Dynamic Symmetry concept; merely ask any competent tailor or dressmaker.

Then St. John tells us that ''the Word was God.'' If this is true and we discover that the Word is cast in the same form as man, who is in God's ''image,'' this system of proportion cannot then be taken lightly. It would be pleasant and enlightening to devote

24

one's whole life to the analytical study of all passages of the Bible and ultimately to the form of the Bible as a whole. But, alas, this must be left to others. For the present we shall have to content ourselves with the excitement of examining the wonders of one great and widely beloved passage.

Some may wish to see Dynamic Symmetry in application in other works except the Bible. They may find it rewarding to examine Aesop's Fables for literary models, one of which is discussed at the end of this book; the Beethoven sonatas and symphonies in music, and almost any great painting. Of course, nobody can afford to overlook the Harmonic Series: here Dynamic Symmetry is demonstrated with absolute mathematical accuracy and in its most clear cut and exact form.

But, this matter of the Harmonic Series brings up a slightly distressing question: can God really enjoy the praises that we sing to Him on Sundays to the dubious accompaniment of an organ that operates in tempered tuning? While we must admit that any such doubt never seemed to deter or inhibit the great Johann Sebastian Bach, we still cannot help but wonder just a bit. And it does seem, upon reflection, that tempered tuning does tend to "commit adultery" with nature's impeccably perfect pitch relationships.

CHAPTER III

Before turning to the conversation between Jesus and the opinionated oft-wedded Samaritan woman, we have to ask what may appear at first glance to be a rude and irreligious question. But, in all sincerity, who could have overheard this conversation and have written it down verbatim?

Although it is not said in so many words, it can safely be assumed that Jesus and the woman were alone during the conversation. According to the story as given in St. John's Gospel, Jesus, weary from a long and taxing journey, sat on Jacob's well while his disciples had gone off to procure some groceries. ("For his disciples were gone away into the city to buy meat").[3] No mention is made of any disciple having remained with Jesus either to keep him company or to serve as his secretary, although such a thing need not necessarily be ruled out as either impossible or improbable.

As for the woman, we read simply, "There cometh a woman from Samaria to draw water."[4] We are not told whether she was alone or accompanied by friends. But it seems quite unlikely that a woman so simple in her living habits as to come herself to a public well to draw water would have a secretary along to record her chance conversations with a stranger who happened to be loitering in the town. Thus, from the scriptural account it seems reasonable to conclude that Jesus and the woman were by themselves, and that no third person was at hand to record and preserve their conversation.

But, even supposing that somebody might have overheard it, is it likely or even conceivable that two strangers passing the time of day at a public well would strike up a conversation of such formal complexity that even the most skilled of writers would be hard put to match it? Is it even remotely possible that

3) John, Chapter 4, v. 8.
4) Ibid., v. 7.

an unplanned conversation would embody structural aspects—recurring ideas at key points, and internal form upon form pyramiding into a great sonata-allegro—that demonstrate almost every conceivable artifice (even a "false" veneer form to conceal the inner mechanism) and time relation technique known to masters of artistic planning? From these considerations it would seem that this familiar passage must be approached as something being considerably more than a simple account of a Biblical incident. The same is true of a great many other apparently simple things, such as a Scriabin Etude, a Bach Invention or a Chorale by Burkhard Waldis.

Did this complexity exist only in this particular passage of the Bible it could be chalked up and dismissed as mere coincidence. But such is not the case. We could have chosen for a model to be examined any of Jesus' other conversations, or the Beatitudes, or the Lord's Prayer, or any of the Psalms, or practically any other significant passage of Scripture and we would have encountered the same kind of planning. In fact, it was not an easy choice to decide upon the present passage as a hub around which to build our book.

Thus, one cannot escape arriving at the conclusion that great and lasting works of art—in whatever medium—derive much of their power from their form and that this form itself "speaks" a silent language to those prepared and willing to understand and "listen."

But it is a curious feature of successful artistic structures that the internal generative form is generally concealed by external features that prevent its being apparent "from the outside." And, even more curious is the fact that analytical text books seem to avoid giving out any practical or pregnant information pertaining to the actual techniques of formal organization as demonstrated by the works they happen to be discussing at the moment.

Take, for example, the great C minor organ Passacaglia by Bach. The almost fantastic complexity resulting from the textural plan in conjunction with the manipulations of the bass as shown in the arrangement of the twenty-one sections (that is, the first unaccompanied statement of the bass and the twenty variations) is largely unmentioned or erroneously analyzed by even the most devoted Bach scholars. And yet, once this form is seen, it is so inevitable; and, being inevitable, it follows that it is inevitably correct and inevitably forceful. And this force created by the form is so great that even a performer who is unaware of its existence cannot entirely suppress its impact.

One of the troubles with formal analysis is that although most forms originate in the same kind of planning, every form is different. Thus, it becomes virtually impossible to discuss the subject of form imformatively except in three ways:

(1) select one model and point out the principles in force with the hope that the reader can apply them elsewhere and in different situations (that is the plan of this book),

(2) discuss in detail the form of every significant artistic composition (but this is impractical because of the magnitude of such a work), or

(3) set forth the principles of formal organization in the abstract with no actual models and leave it to the reader to find his own way (except for the fact that very few students would be able to translate into practical artistic application a purely abstract principle that has not been illustrated).

Of course, to some extent everybody is familiar with the silent language of form in its more obvious manifestations in symbols and emblems. The country's flag, the Cross, the Star of David, the Swastika, the Masonic ''G'', trade-marks of innumerable commodities and services, etc., are all exercises in form and are to some degree generally understood and recognized. So is a building a form, and a dress, and a human body, and a bird in flight, and a cloud, and a rainbow, and a poem. Whatever exists is in a form. It cannot be otherwise; for what is not in a form has no existence and is devoid of any power to effect. But the underlying invisible complex form with which this book is concerned is, perhaps, less obvious and quite possibly less widely appreciated, and less generally subject to being appreciated.

But it is this inner invisible form, akin to the invisible and intangible mathematical ratios that make for a well engineered boat, automobile or airplane, that provides the basis for a successful composition in music, literature, painting or architecture. And without it any artistic structure will only be hollow and of its own weight will collapse.

This awareness seems to bring a person one step closer to a comprehension of the statement in the Nicene Creed, "I believe...in all things visible and invisible." And, to a large degree, the difference between the "visible" and the "invisible" lies in the perception and understanding of the viewer or listener.

CHAPTER IV

Let us now turn to the passage we have selected to serve as basis for our observations on form as it appears in the fourth chapter St. John's Gospel (verses 7-26):

[1001]   **CHAPTER 4**

Jesus Talks with a Woman of Samaria

WHEN therefore the Lord knew how the Pharisees had heard that Jesus made and baptized more disciples than John,

2 (Though Jesus himself baptized not, but his disciples,)

3 He left Judæa, and departed again into Galilee.

4 And he must needs go through Sâ-mā'rĭ-à.

5 Then cometh he to a city of Sâ-mā'rĭ-à, which is called Sȳ'-chär, near to the parcel of ground *that Jacob gave to his son Joseph.

6 Now Jacob's well was there. Jesus therefore, being wearied with *his* journey, sat thus on the well: *and* it was about the sixth hour.

7 There cometh a woman of Sâ-mā'rĭ-à to draw water: Jesus saith unto her, Give me to drink.

8 (For his disciples were gone away unto the city to buy meat.)

9 Then saith the woman of Sâ-mā'rĭ-à unto him, How is it that thou, being a Jew, askest drink of me, which am a woman of Sâ-mā'rĭ-à? for *the Jews have no dealings with the Samaritans.

10 Jesus answered and said unto her, If thou knewest *the gift of God, and who it is that saith to thee, Give me to drink; thou wouldest have asked of him, and he would have given thee *living water.

11 The woman saith unto him, Sir, thou hast nothing to draw with, and the well is deep: from whence then hast thou that living water?

12 Art thou greater than our father Jacob, which gave us the well, and drank thereof himself, and his children, and his cattle?

13 Jesus answered and said unto her, Whosoever drinketh of this water shall thirst again:

14 But *whosoever drinketh of the water that I shall give him shall never thirst; but the water that I shall give him *shall be in him a well of water springing up into everlasting life.

Marginal references:
c ch. 7:16
d Col. 1:19
e Dan. 7:14 Heb. 2:8
f Hab. 2:4 Rom. 1:17
g Gal. 3:10
4 Or, *take unto himself*

CHAP. 4
a Gen. 33:19 Gen. 48:22 Josh. 24:32
b 2 Kin. 17:24 Ezra 4:3 Acts 10:28
c Is. 9:6 Is. 42:6 Rom. 8:32
d Is. 12:3 Is. 44:3 Jer. 2:13 Zech. 13:1 Zech. 14:8
e ch. 6:35
f ch. 7:38

30

15 The *woman saith unto him, Sir, give me this water, that I thirst not, neither come hither to draw.

16 Jesus saith unto her, Go, call thy husband, and come hither.

17 The woman answered and said, I have no husband. Jesus said unto her, Thou hast well said, I have no husband:

18 For thou hast had five husbands; and he whom thou now hast is not thy husband: in that saidst thou truly.

19 The woman saith unto him, Sir, *I perceive that thou art a prophet.

20 Our fathers worshipped *in this mountain; and ye say, that in *Jerusalem is the place where men ought to worship.

21 Jesus saith unto her, Woman, believe me, the hour cometh, when *ye shall neither in this mountain, nor yet at Jerusalem, worship the Father.

22 Ye worship *ye know not what: we know what we worship: for *salvation is of the Jews.

23 But the hour cometh, and now is, when the true worshippers shall worship the Father in *spirit and in *truth: for the Father seeketh such to worship him.

24 God *is a Spirit: and they that worship him must worship *him* in spirit and in truth.

25 The woman saith unto him, I know that *Mĕs-sī'as cometh, which is called Christ: when he is come, he will tell us all things.

26 Jesus saith unto her, *I that speak unto thee am *he*.

27 ¶And upon this came his disciples, and marvelled that he talked with the woman: yet no man said, What seekest thou? or, Why talkest thou with her?

28 The woman then left her
1248

A. D. 30

CHAP. 4

g Rom. 6:
23
1 John 5:
20

h Luke 7:
16

i Gen. 12:6
Judg. 9:7

j Deut. 12:
5
2 Chr. 7:
12

k Mal. 1:11
1 Tim. 2:
8

l 2 Kin.
17:29

m Is. 2:3
Luke 24:
47
Rom. 9:4,
5

n ch. 14:17
Rom. 8:4
1 Cor. 3:
16
1 Cor. 6:
17
Gal. 5:25
Phil. 3:3

o ch. 1:17

p Acts 17:
24-29
2 Cor. 3:
17

q Deut. 18:
15
Dan. 9:24

r Mark 14:
61
ch. 9:37
ch. 10:36

s Job 23:12
ch. 6:38
ch. 17:4
ch. 19:30

t Matt. 9:
37
Luke 10:
2

u Ps. 19:11
Ps. 58:11
Prov. 11:
18
Dan. 12:
3
1 Cor. 3:8
James 5:
20
2 John 8

v Acts 10:
43
1 Pet. 1:
12

w Gen. 49:
10

x Gen. 32:
26

y Is. 42:1
Rom. 15:
8

z ch. 17:8
1 John 4:
14

waterpot, and went her way into the city, and saith to the men,

29 Come, see a man, which told me all things that ever I did: is not this the Christ?

30 Then they went out of the city, and came unto him.

31 ¶In the mean while his disciples prayed him, saying, Master, eat.

32 But he said unto them, I have meat to eat that ye know not of.

33 Therefore said the disciples one to another, Hath any man brought him *ought* to eat?

34 Jesus saith unto them, *My meat is to do the will of him that sent me, and to finish his work.

35 Say not ye, There are yet four months, and *then* cometh harvest? behold, I say unto you, Lift up your eyes, and look on the fields; for *they are white already to harvest.

36 And he that reapeth *receiveth wages, and gathereth fruit unto life eternal: that both he that soweth and he that reapeth may rejoice together.

37 And herein is that saying true, One soweth, and another reapeth.

38 I sent you to reap that whereon ye bestowed no labour: *other men laboured, and ye are entered into their labours.

39 ¶And *many of the Samaritans of that city believed on him for the saying of the woman, which testified, He told me all that ever I did.

40 So *when the Samaritans were come unto him, they besought him that he would tarry with them: and he abode there two days.

41 And *many more believed because of his own word;

42 And said unto the woman, Now we believe, not because of thy saying: for *we have heard

31

No presentation of a complicated form could be more subtle. The underlying generative structure makes itself felt. However, visually as given in the Bible the dialogue is deceptively divided into verses and is interspersed with parenthetical comments so that its innermost design is concealed rather than made apparent to the eye. But this can be remedied merely by writing out the conversation in the manner of a play. In this format the Dynamic Symmetry planning begins to shine through, and the first observation is that the dialogue is cast within the confines of a 34-idea framework. And 34, it will be recalled from Chapter II, is the *ninth* number in the Dynamic Symmetry series when the two ones are used at the beginning.

JESUS: 1. (1) Give me to drink.

WOMAN: 2. *(1) How is it that thou, being a Jew, askest drink of me, which am a woman of Samaria? for*
3. *(2) the Jews have no dealings with the Samaritans.*

JESUS: 4. (2) If thou knewest the gift of God, and who it is that saith to thee, Give me to drink; thou wouldest have asked of him, and
5. (3) he would have given thee living water.

WOMAN: 6. *(3) Sir, thou hast nothing to draw with, and*
7. *(4) the well is deep:*
8. *(5) from whence then hast thou that living water?*
9. *(6) Art thou greater than our father Jacob, which gave us the well,*
    and drank thereof himself,
    and his children,
    and his cattle?

JESUS: 10. (4) Whosoever drinketh of this water shall thirst again: But
11. (5) whosoever drinketh of the water that I shall give him shall never thirst; but
12. (6) the water that I shall give him shall be in him a well of water springing up into everlasting life.

WOMAN: 13. *(7) Sir, give me this water, that I thirst not,*
14. *(8) neither come hither to draw.*
JESUS: 15. (7) Go, call thy husband, and
16. (8) come hither.
WOMAN: 17. *(9) I have no husband.*
JESUS: 18. (9) Thou hast well said, I have no husband: for
19.(10) thou hast had five husbands; and
20.(11) he whom thou now hast is not thy husband:
21.(12) in that saidst thou truly.
WOMAN: 22.*(10) Sir, I perceive that thou art a prophet.*
23.*(11) Our fathers worshipped in this mountain; and*
24.*(12) ye say, that in Jerusalem is the place where*
men ought to worship.
JESUS: 25.(13) Woman, believe me, the hour cometh, when ye
shall neither in this mountain, not yet at Jerusalem, worship the Father.

26.(14) Ye worship ye know not what:
27.(15) we know what we worship: for
28.(16) salvation is of the Jews.
29.(17) But the hour cometh, and now is, when the true
worshippers shall worship the Father in spirit
and in truth: for
30.(18) the Father seeketh such to worship him.
31.(19) God is a Spirit: and
32.(20) they that worship him must worship him in spirit
and in truth.
WOMAN: 33.(13) *I know that Messias cometh, which is called*
Christ: when he is come, he will tell us all
things.
JESUS: 34.(21) I that speak unto thee am he.

The woman has two multiple statements; her sixth in which
she lists all who drank from the well, and her thirteenth wherein
she tells what she knows about Messias.

Thirty-four as a number has been a source of widespread
fascination and it might be interesting to examine one significant
instance at this time. But, first, it can be applicable symbol-

33

ically to Jesus' life, ministry and resurrection in rather a challenging manner, which some readers may see fit to dispute or reject.

It is a widely accepted tradition—based primarily on apocryphal writings and for which no clearcut supporting scriptural evidence can be offered—that Jesus' earthly life closed on the cross at the age of thirty-three. Thus, it is not too farfetched to take thirty-four as a symbolic representation of his appearances after the resurrection. Consider Jesus' final statement in his conversation with the Samaritan woman—the thirty-fourth—wherein he says without qualification, "I that speak unto thee am he." (That is, the Messias.) It is just this assertion that was proved by Jesus' resurrection!

A similar symbolic representation exists in the form in the Crucifixus of Bach's Mass in B minor. This consists of fourteen variations (or more accurately, sections) over a ground bass, one for each Station of the Cross. And just as the plan of the fourteen Stations depicts thirteen incidents *above* the ground and one *below* the ground, namely the burial, so Bach's symbolic form for the setting of "Crucifixus etiam pro nobis sub Pontio Pilato et sepultus est."[5] contains thirteen sections over the four-bar ground bass in the key of E minor, while the fourteenth is merely a single closing major chord on G. It is doubly symbolic that while each of the thirteen painful scenes above the ground is brought to a close, the depicting of the ultimate peace as implied by the burial is never developed. Only one *major* chord represents the fourteenth Station.

Thus, if we may be permitted to use Bach's form as a valid parallel, the formal symbolism of Jesus' declaration of himself as the Messias in the thirty-fourth statement is quite within the bounds of reasonable employment of symbolism through form.

But, thirty-four as a number has had several other interesting uses; far too many, in fact, to mention here. One instance will suffice for the present. In Dürer's painting entitled "Melancolia" this diagram, a so-called magic square, appears as an ornament on the wall (see frontispiece):

5) "And was crucified also for us under Pontius Pilate; He suffered and was buried."

34

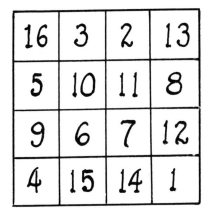

16	3	2	13
5	10	11	8
9	6	7	12
4	15	14	1

Its construction is achieved quite simply, merely by arranging the numbers from 1 to 16 into four interlocking triangles, thus:

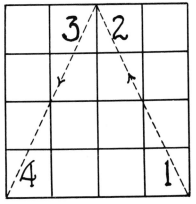
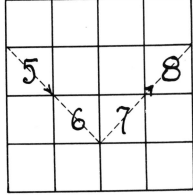

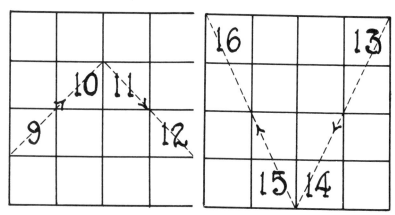

These numbers, so arranged, bring 34 into play arithmetically in eighteen different ways. The first ten come about by the addition of the numbers in each vertical, horizontal and diagonal column.

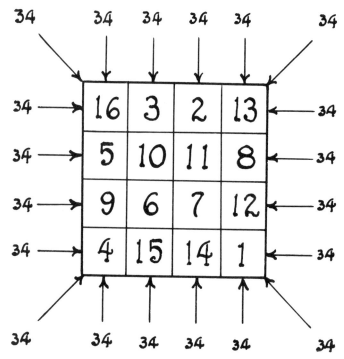

Four times more the sum of 34 is achieved by adding the numbers in each of the four quarters.

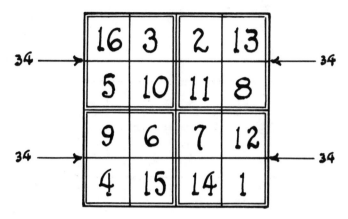

Still another 34 occurs in the central square of four numbers.

16	3	2	13
5	10	11	8
9	6	7	12
4	15	14	1

Two more sums of 34 exist in two sets of opposite pairs, and these when viewed together combine to form a cross.

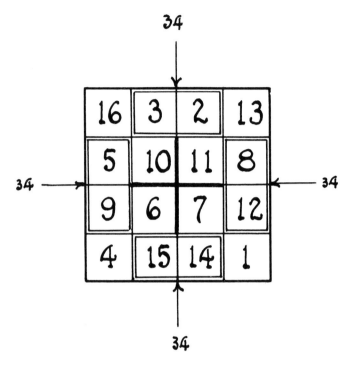

Finally, the four corner numbers add up to 34.

16	3	2	13
5	10	11	8
9	6	7	12
4	15	14	1

Besides the above eighteen ways in which 34 is achieved by means of adding numbers according to various symmetrical arrangements, we find that in each quarter vertically aligned pairs of numbers bring into play the 13 : 21 relationship of the Dynamic Symmetry series.

$$21 : 13 \qquad 13 : 21$$

16	3	2	13
5	10	11	8
9	6	7	12
4	15	14	1

$$13 : 21 \qquad 21 : 13$$

Still other symmetrical appearances of the 13 : 21 ratio can be found, but for the present we will point out only two more—in a right angle—and leave it to the reader to amuse himself by finding other interesting and significant numerical patterns for himself.

$$21 \quad : \quad 13$$

16	3	2	13
5	10	11	8
9	6	7	12
4	15	14	1

13 : 21

Then, by subtracting the 13 from the 21, each of these arrangements show a difference of 8. Thus, we can demonstrate the interweaving of the 8 : 13 : 21 : 34 ratio plan in numerous ways within the one design originating in two pairs of inverted triangles within a square.

What does all this prove? To some people absolutely nothing; to others it is merely an arithmetical curiosity, but to a third group it provides a clue to the thinking of one of the great artists of all time. This last group will see it, perhaps, as a symbol of a craving for perfection of a whole, as well as in every part and in every direction and interlocking dimension within the whole.

But, the appalling degree in which the implications of symbols of this nature elude even some who ought to understand them is shown by a respected textbook on art in which this diagram is described as a "calendar"!

Much more could be said about 34 and many more examples could be cited that demonstrate its uses in symbolic representation, but these few assorted observations will suffice to show that the brief conversation between Jesus and his Samaritan friend is cast in a form, the dimensions of which are in effect a chest designed to house a multiplicity of structural wonders, which we shall undertake to examine in some detail in the chapters that follow. Thus, we arrive at a consideration of tremendous importance in the building of any artistic structure: its over-all scope and dimensions *must* be an integral part of the form itself, and not merely a hit-or-miss happenstance. This is equally true whether the content of the form consists of ideas, melodies, figures or spaces as in a building.

For the painter, sculptor or architect this is a relatively matter-of-course thing since the dimensions within which they operate are often governed by conditions not of their own choice or making. But, for a composer it presents more of a problem; except under certain conditions such as in the writing of incidental music for a film, he is not ordinarily bound to any predetermined time span of exact duration. Thus, there is always the temptation to a composer to "weave along" with his material until he has used up what he has to say.

But the great and lasting works of the musical literature appear to have been conceived and executed within predetermined dimensions whether these were originally thought of in terms of measures or as time spans. Of course, in a variation form such as a Passacaglia this is inevitable and not too noteworthy, but it becomes of paramount importance in formal mechanisms of great complexity such as Palestrina's *Stabat Mater* or in a Beethoven sonata-allegro.

For a teacher of musical composition, the necessity and advisability of thinking out a form as to its outermost limits is one of the most difficult things to "put across" to students who have not matured to this degree of form awareness. In fact, many composers never come to a realization of this necessity, and great numbers of communicatively inferior compositions come about as a result of it.

CHAPTER V

In Chapter II, when the Dynamic Symmetry principle was introduced, it was pointed out how by preceding the Fibonacci Series with an introductory 1, the 1 : 1 ratio would result. In other words, this would show a given form cut in half. Thereby a background comes into being against which the Dynamic Symmetry divisions will operate in a sort of third dimensional perspective.

In every medium of art the mid-point, or fulcrum on which the form balances, has been the subject of much careful attention. Musical examples can be cited in abundance. In his celebrated *Stabat Mater* Palestrina shows the exact middle by letting all eight parts sing "Mater." In the first movement of Beethoven's ingenious Piano Sonata No. 1 in F minor, the middle is disguised by an eight measure passage which—unburdened by melody—serves as a kind of overlay to conceal the structural division. Reger, in the organ Passacaglia in D minor, casts his middle variation—the seventh in a thirteen section form—in an idiom quite unlike its context; and Bach does essentially the same thing in the eleventh of his twenty-one sections in the C minor Organ Passacaglia.

For sheer and unsurpassed ingenuity, in Bach's 371 Chorale harmonizations, each of the 2265 lines closed by a fermata is marked off by some subtle harmonic or contrapuntal device, an unexpected dissonance, a low or high point in some voice or any one of a variety of things that would occur only to a Johann Sebastian Bach. And, in paintings of the Last Supper, the scene customarily consists of thirteen characters, with Jesus in the middle.

Turning to the realm of music theory, the midpoint of any key—namely, the tritone from the tonic—is the leading-tone of the dominant key and thereby is the instrument that lifts the listener to the next level of tonality within the circle of fifths, thereby supplying the essential technique for the whole art of modulation.

Now, what exactly takes place at the middle of the conversation between Jesus and the woman of Samaria? It being a 34-idea form, there is no central idea and no mid-point as such, so the 17th and 18th ideas must of necessity flank the middle. In the 17th idea the woman says quite simply and without further elaboration, "I have no husband"; and in the 18th idea Jesus assures her that she is quite correct in saying "I have no husband," thereby quoting her four word declarative sentence without alteration.

But, this is not all. For both the woman and Jesus it is their *ninth* statement in the conversation. Thus, the precise middle is marked of as follows:

WOMAN: 17 *(9) I have no husband.*
JESUS: 18 (9) Thou hast well said, I have no husband:

This makes three times so far that we have come up against the number 9: twice here and once in the fact that 34 is the *ninth* number of the Dynamic Symmetry series.

Inasmuch as this book is concerned with form in the technical sense and, as far as possible aims at keeping aloof from symbolic interpretation we shall offer nothing in the way of mystical or spiritual interpretations either of the number 9 or of the repetition of the phrase, "I have no husband."

This number, although not in the Dynamic Symmetry series, often enters into formal calculations either as the square of 3, or as a byproduct of other relationships and invariably as the first idea in the closing five-idea section of a thirteen-unit form as in broaching the description of the unpleasant state of the ungodly in Psalm 1.

Nine is also to be found serving as the foundation of games: Baseball being played by two *nine*-man teams in a *nine*-inning game. But there is a much older game, Nine Men's Morris, to which Shakespeare refers in *A Midsummer Night's Dream*. In Act

43

II, Scene I, Titania, lamenting "the forgeries of jealousy," observes that

> The nine men's morris is fill'd up with mud;
> And the quaint mazes in the wanton green,
> For lack of tread, are undistinguishable:

Nine Men's Morris is played on a mill board which consists of three concentric squares joined by four transversals so that there are 24 points of contact.

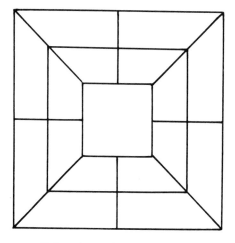

This "quaint maze" has been found on the steps of the Acropolis at Athens, on the deck of a Viking vessel and on a tombstone on the Isle of Man in the Irish Sea. It has come down from the most ancient times in the cultures of India and China, amongst many African tribes and on the Amazon. It is said to have been played by shepherds in western Asia for centuries before the time of Homer.

In the realm of philosophy there are the celebrated six Enneads, or nine-groups, of Plotinus. Curiously enough, this six-fold nine-group arrangement of Plotinus' writings grouped into three volumes—an ingenious study of form—was made by his pupil Porphyry, the third century antagonist of the Christians. The entire list of the topics discussed therein are given herewith in full to demonstrate how the concept of form can be employed to organize thoughts and ideas on a large scale much as is done in the comparatively short excerpt from St. John's Gospel that we have chosen for examination.

PORPHYRY'S TOPICAL ARRANGEMENT
OF PLOTINUS' WORKS

Volume First—Universal or General

FIRST ENNEAD—Psychological ethics
1. About the Conception of the Living Being and of Man.
2. About the Virtues.
3. About Dialectics.
4. About Happiness.
5. Whether Happiness consists of Permanency?
6. Concerning Beauty.
7. About the First-Good and the other Goods.
8. About the Origin of Evil.
9. About the Rational Exit from Life, or Suicide.

SECOND ENNEAD—Physical and Cosmical
1. About the World.
2. About Circular Motion.
3. About the Effectiveness and Influence of the Stars.
4. About the two kinds of Matter.
5. About Energy and Force.
6. About Quality and Form.
7. About the Commingling Penetrating All.
8. Why Distant Objects appear smaller.
9. Against those (Gnostics) who assume an evil World-Creator and who consider the world evil.

SIXTH ENNEAD—The Existent, Good, One

Many interpretations and applications of the number 9 are to be found in other quarters; to mention a few at random one can note that a nine-month span precedes the birth of a child; Milton writes about "nine-fold Harmony"; that there were nine muses, and in Winnetka, Illinois, the Bahai organization has built a magnificent nine-sided symbolic edifice to house its gatherings and activities.

So, for anyone interested in pursuing the number 9 further in its symbolism and application, there are many paths and byways to follow.

CHAPTER VI

The first lesson the creative artist must learn about form is that no work of art can function effectively or even exist as a structural organism within one single form. Simplicity is the sum total of complexity. This can be illustrated quite simply in any ordinary day of living.

The twenty-four-hour time span is "divided" by nature into daylight and darkness. This is a constantly varying division since day by day the seasons move from the shortest day of the year to the longest, and vice versa. Yet, against this division of the day we superimpose—each according to his own needs and desires—another division of the day consisting of periods given over to sleeping and waking, which usually do not coincide with the natural division into daylight and darkness. And, the period allotted for being awake is further subdivided into smaller segments for working, playing, eating, worshipping, helping one's neighbor, etc., etc.

An everyday evidence of a double form is in the realm of ladies' fashions. From season to season the dress designers move the "waistline" up or down according to the dictates of the current styles. But, this is an entirely artificial "waistline." The natural waistline, like the natural division between daylight and darkness, is *not* movable—nor, in fact, is it visible. But, there it is, nonetheless!

This, however, is not to disparage the work of dress designers; theirs is a great art. Theirs is the task either to reveal the human figure as in the case of a cabaret singer's gown, or to conceal it as in a nun's habit. But, the more the designer is charged with the objective of concealing the human figure, the more he must construct an artificial external form; and the more artificial the form, the more his artistry and use of proportions comes into play. It is lack of skill and poverty of artistry in this direction that makes for those well-meant but unfortunately "homemade" looking garments.

48

So, in the conversation between Jesus and the Samaritan woman there is an external form, dividing the 34-idea dialogue into two parts of fourteen and twenty ideas which is *not* in itself a Dynamic Symmetry ratio. In fact it is only 1.429 as against 1.618, taken on a purely arithmetical basis. This division occurs where Jesus abruptly changes the subject of the conversation and commands the woman, "Go, call thy husband," bringing about an external veneer form as follows:

JESUS: 1.   (1) Give me to drink.

WOMAN: 2.   *(1) How is it that thou, being a Jew, askest drink of me, which am a woman of Samaria? for*

          3.   *(2) the Jews have no dealings with the Samaritans.*

JESUS: 4.   (2) If thou knewest the gift of God, and who it is that saith to thee, Give me to drink; thou wouldest have asked of him, and

          5.   (3) he would have given thee living water.

WOMAN: 6.   *(3) Sir, thou hast nothing to draw with, and*

          7.   *(4) the well is deep:*

          8.   *(5) from whence then hast thou that living water?*

          9.   *(6) Art thou greater than our father Jacob, which gave us the well,*
                and drank thereof himself,
                and his children,
                and his cattle?

JESUS: 10.   (4) Whosoever drinketh of this water shall thirst again: But

       11.   (5) whosoever drinketh of the water that I shall give him shall never thirst; but

       12.   (6) the water that I shall give him shall be in him a well of water springing up into everlasting life.

WOMAN: 13.   *(7) Sir, give me this water, that I thirst not,*

       14.   *(8) neither come hither to draw.*

JESUS: 15.   (7) Go, call thy husband, and

       16.   (8) come hither.

WOMAN: 17.   *(9) I have no husband.*

JESUS: 18. (9) Thou hast well said, I have no husband: for
        19. (10) thou hast had five husbands; and
        20. (11) he whom thou now hast is not thy husband:
        21. (12) in that saidst thou truly.
WOMAN: 22. *(10) Sir, I perceive that thou art a prophet.*
        23. *(11) Our fathers worshipped in this mountain; and*
        24. *(12) ye say, that in Jerusalem is the place where*
            men ought to worship.
JESUS: 25. (13) Woman, believe me, the hour cometh, when ye
            shall neither in this mountain, not yet at Jeru-
            salem, worship the Father.
        26. (14) Ye worship ye know not what:
        27. (15) we know what we worship: for
        28. (16) salvation is of the Jews.
        29. (17) But the hour cometh, and now is, when the true
            worshippers shall worship the Father in spirit
            and in truth: for
        30. (18) the Father seeketh such to worship him.
        31. (19) God is a Spirit: and
        32. (20) they that worship him must worship him in
            spirit and in truth.
WOMAN: 33. *(13) I know that Messias cometh, which is called*
            Christ: when he is come, he will tell us all
            things.
JESUS: 34. (21) I that speak unto thee am he.

External forms serve a useful purpose; and, in fact, are the
means of conveying to the auditor or viewer the over-all total concept intended by the artist. The student of musical composition
must learn that the melody—the part of a structure that appeals
to and is recognized by the listener—is often merely an icing,
technically speaking, designed to ornament a systematically
constructed formal plan of harmony. And, it might shock some
musicians to learn that the often maligned "second fiddle" is not
infrequently more important structurally—in terms of composi-
tional technique—than his more distinguished and sometimes
better paid colleague, the first violinist.

Similarly, in the construction of an automobile, the eye-catching external design — the instrument for attracting and appealing to the purchaser — is entirely subservient to and dependent upon the engineer's tussle with cold and abstract mathematical ratios that make the car perform safely and efficiently, but which, like the mythical dilly bird, are "neither seen nor heard-o."

A most interesting musical composition that illustrates this principle is Felix Mendelssohn's familiar and well-beloved song, "O, for the Wings of a Dove." Here over a rigidly calculated structural form divided according to a highly advanced application of Dynamic Symmetry, the solo voice sings a lyrical line so fluid in contour and spirit that at times it almost sounds like a free improvisation.

Therefore, while Jesus' conversation with the Samaritan woman contains many formal wonders which interlock beneath the surface, as it were, we could not proceed with our examination of the internal mechanisms of the passage without first pausing for a moment or two to consider the external veneer form, which— after all—may be the most apparent division to the reader.

CHAPTER VII

We are now prepared to examine the complex inner mechanism of interlocking forms operating concurrently, as it were, beneath the external surface form pointed out in the preceding chapter. In so doing, we shall endeavor to follow a consistent course of working down through the Dynamic Symmetry series. We have already come upon a few interesting things pertaining to 34 as an entity and the two ones at the beginning of the series.

Our model containing the noon-day conversation between Jesus and the Samaritan woman features a thirteen-idea "octave" at either end of the form. Thus, our first observations concerning the inner forms is that there exists a two-fold demonstration of the 13 : 21 ratio, in that the thirteen-idea "octave" at the end reverses it into 21 : 13. In other words, the 13 : 21 division runs against itself in retrograde.

The first 13-idea "octave" is arranged as follows:

JESUS: 1. (1) Give me to drink.

WOMAN: 2. *(1) How is it that thou, being a Jew, askest drink of me, which am a woman of Samaria? for*

           3. *(2) the Jews have no dealings with the Samaritans.*

JESUS: 4. (2) If thou knewest the gift of God, and who it is that saith to thee, Give me to drink; thou wouldest have asked of him, and

           5. (3) he would have given thee living water.

WOMAN: 6. *(3) Sir, thou hast nothing to draw with, and*

           7. *(4) the well is deep:*

           8. *(5) from whence then hast thou that living water?*

           9. *(6) Art thou greater than our father Jacob, which gave us the well,*
                    and drank thereof himself,
                    and his children,
                    and his cattle?

JESUS: 10. (4) Whosoever drinketh of this water shall thirst again: But
11. (5) whosoever drinketh of the water that I shall give him shall never thirst; but
12. (6) the water that I shall give him shall be in him a well of water springing up into everlasting life.
WOMAN: 13. *(7) Sir, give me this water, that I thirst not,*

Several interesting things occur in this passage. Ideas 1 and 13, corresponding to the two tonics of a chromatic scale, are significantly related. In idea 1 Jesus requests by means of an imperative sentence without qualification, "Give me to drink." In idea 13, the request is reversed as the woman asks of Jesus, "Sir, give me this water, that I thirst not." Incidentally, this thirteenth idea is the last mention of "water" by either Jesus or the woman in the entire conversation.

The closing thirteen-idea "octave," while quite different internally, is surprisingly similar in the terminal ideas. Here the "octave" begins at idea 22 with the woman's awareness of Jesus' uniqueness, "Sir, I perceive that thou art a prophet." It closes at the 34th idea with Jesus' acknowledgement that "I that speak unto thee am he." Thus, as in the first 13-idea "octave" the two tonics represented a transferral of direction from Jesus to the woman, so in the closing 13-idea "octave" the two tonics represent the woman's perception and Jesus' acknowledgement.

WOMAN: 22. *(10) Sir, I perceive that thou art a prophet.*
23. *(11) Our fathers worshipped in this mountain; and*
24. *(12) ye say, that in Jerusalem is the place where men ought to worship.*
JESUS: 25. (13) Woman, believe me, the hour cometh, when ye shall neither in this mountain, not yet at Jerusalem, worship the Father.
26. (14) Ye worship ye know not what:
27. (15) we know what we worship: for

28. (16) salvation is of the Jews.
29. (17) But the hour cometh, and now is, when the true worshippers shall worship the Father in spirit and in truth: for
30. (18) the Father seeketh such to worship him.
31. (19) God is a Spirit: and
32. (20) they that worship him must worship him in spirit and in truth.

WOMAN: 33. *(13) I know that Messias cometh, which is called Christ: when he is come, he will tell us all things.*

JESUS: 34. (21) I that speak unto thee am he.

It may come as a surprise to some to find that a 13-idea form is called an "octave". This is due to the fact that while the term "octave" ordinarily refers to the 8-note diatonic scale, the same terminal interval also contains the thirteen notes of the chromatic scale, thus

C, c-sharp, d, e-flat, e, F, f-sharp, G, a-flat, a, b-flat, b, C.

Within this 13-note octave lies every harmony, every concord, every discord, every modulation that exists in music as we know it. This all-inclusiveness of the octave is the reason why so many philosophical and occult teachings are either based upon or demonstrated in terms of the musical scale. In fact, some have gone so far as to show their conception of the whole plan of the universe by means of the musical scale. And from century to century the scale continues to be a pregnant source of thought and experiment.

This, then enables us to show the points of division that set off the first Dynamic Symmetry ratios of this text that bring into play the two 13-idea terminal octaves by means of the following diagram.

54

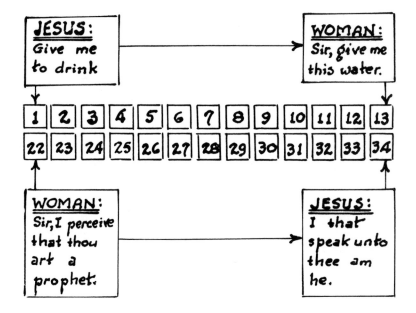

For the writers of the Bible, the 13-idea form was often useful. Psalms 1, 23 and 150 are outstanding examples. A superb musical setting of Psalm 150 by Cesar Franck illustrates perfectly the form of that text. The Psalm is divided into five ideas telling *why* and *where* to praise the Lord and *eight* ideas telling *how* to praise Him. Consequently, Franck's music for the first five ideas is notably different from the music of the last eight.

Many other things are grouped in units or multiples of thirteen. Typical of the Passacaglia form is the well-known one in D minor for organ by the learned German composer Max Reger, which as was mentioned in a previous chapter, is in thirteen sections. The year contains 52 weeks, and there are 52 playing cards in a pack. Both demonstrate an even multiple of thirteen. Tarot cards on the other hand, come in packs of 78—a higher multiple of thirteen. Pictures of the Last Supper always contain thirteen characters—Jesus and his twelve deciples. And for some superstitious folk, thirteen has definitely unpleasant connotations. Observations on thirteen as either a structural or metaphysical entity could continue far beyond the limits of this slim volume, and for anyone interested in this matter much has been written on and about it.

But, before leaving this subject, it might be well to add that sometimes two consecutive numbers can stand for the same thing. This principle can be illustrated very simply by pointing out that a row of thirteen houses would be separated by twelve lawns. And since the twelve lawns are not possible without the thirteen houses twelve and thirteen in a sense stand for the the same thing.

The celebrated Russian composer and theorist Sergei Ivanovich Taneiev wrote a famous treatise on Convertible Counterpoint wherein he numbers intervals according to the distances between the intermediate notes rather than according to the intermediate notes themselves as is the custom in this country. For instance, we would call the interval from C to F a 4th because of the terminal notes of C and F and the intermediate notes of D and E, thus:

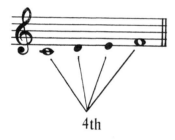

4th

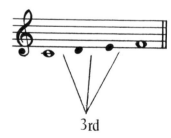

3rd

But Taneiev would call it a third because of the number of intervals between the four notes.

In the calculation of Double Counterpoint this makes some difference in the definition and solution of a problem. For instance, in what we in this country call Double Counterpoint at the 10th, we come to the curious arithmetical oddity that

56

6 + 5 equals 10. But, by the Taneiev system this would be Double Counterpoint at the 9th and the inversion would indicate that 5 + 4 equals 9. Of course, all this is only on paper and has not the slightest effect on the sound.

These last observations about the possible symbolic equality of two adjacent numbers is purely parenthetical and has no real application in the conversation between Jesus and the Samaritan woman. But it does apply in some of the less familiar Old Testament and Apocryphal texts. In music it applies in some cases where themes or episodic sections overlap rather than merely follow one another.

CHAPTER VIII

The two terminal thirteen-idea "octaves" pointed out in the preceding chapter must be examined in three different ways—first, for Jesus' sayings; secondly for what the woman said; and, finally, for the combination of what Jesus and the woman both said. In the present chapter we shall look rather in some detail at the arrangements of ideas as Jesus said them.

The first observation is an obvious one: the opening thirteen-idea "octave" contains six statements by Jesus;

1. (1) Give me to drink.

4. (2) If thou knewest the gift of God, and who it is that saith to thee, Give me to drink; thou wouldst have asked of him, and
5. (3) he would have given thee living water.

10. (4) Whosoever drinketh of this water shall thirst again: But
11. (5) whosoever drinketh of the water that I shall give him shall never thirst; but
12. (6) the water that I shall give him shall be in him a well of water springing up into everlasting life.

while the closing "octave" of the same numerical dimensions contains nine statements by Jesus.

25. (13) Woman, believe me, the hour cometh, when ye shall neither in this mountain, nor yet at Jerusalem, worship the Father.
26. (14) Ye worship ye know not what:
27. (15) we know what we worship: for
28. (16) salvation is of the Jews.
29. (17) But the hour cometh, and now is, when the true worshippers shall worship the Father in spirit and in truth: for

30. (18) the Father seeketh such to worship him.
31. (19) God is a Spirit: and
32. (20) they that worship him must worship him in spirit and in truth.

34. (21) I that speak unto thee am he.

Thus, so far as Jesus' utterances are concerned we find a 6 to 9 (or 2:3 tripled) ratio between the two terminal thirteen-idea "octaves,"

The six statements in the opening "octave" intermingle to form a veritable web of the lowest Dynamic Symmetry ratios. To begin with, the very arrangement of these statements—divided, as it were, by those of the woman—are according to the Fibonacci series as follows: 1 : 2 : 3
              statement   statements   statements

The ratio 1:2 occurs in several ways. First, two statements contain the sentence "Give me to drink," while the remaining four feature the word "water." Thus, through two and four we encounter the 1:2 ratio doubled.

The same 1:2 ratio occurs twice in the last three statements; i.e., (4), (5) and (6) by Jesus, but here it is not doubled. One idea speaks of "this water," that is the physical water in Jacob's well, while two refer to Jesus' mystical water. On the other hand, as shown in the lower portion of the following diagram, two ideas have as the subject of the sentence, "Whosoever drinketh of . . . water," while the last idea makes no mention of drinking.

The multiple plan of these six statements can be readily shown in the accompanying two-fold diagram.

It will be observed from this two-fold diagram, but not necessarily from a reading of the text itself, that from the formal point of view there is a good deal of activity at Jesus' fifth statement. It is the central idea, or fulcrum, of the closing triad of ideas spoken by Jesus within the first thirteen-idea "octave" which embodies the concurrently operating 1:2 and 2:1 ratios as explained above. Moreover, this emphasis on the

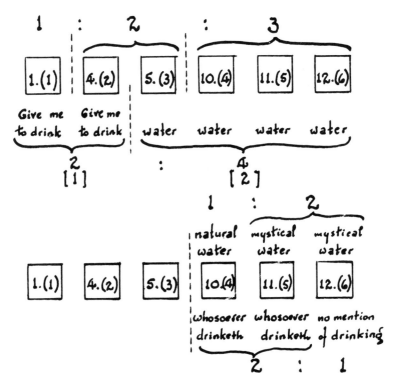

fifth idea together with its change of meaning, sets it and the subsequent idea apart from the preceding four, thereby bringing into play the 4 : 2 (or 2 : 1 doubled) ratio.

This last noted division is brought about also by another device that was characteristic of the Biblical authors; namely, the use of practically the same wording for both the positive and negative meanings,

10. (4) Whosoever drinketh of this water shall thirst.
11. (5) Whosoever drinketh of . . . water . . . shall . . . thirst.

Two such similarly worded statements are often used to mark off a division in the form. At the middle of the dialogue, "I have no husband," serves the same purpose. And, in Psalm 150, a formal division is achieved by two almost identical ideas in "Praise him upon the loud cymbals": and "praise him upon the high sounding cymbals."

In strict academic Counterpoint the repetition of a note is forbidden in any situation when two or more notes are written against one note in the cantus firmus, especially if the earlier of the two notes is accented. This is so because repeated notes set up a division, or in technical contrapuntal parlance, a "dead" interval; and elementary counterpoint exercises usually feature only "live" intervals. Such a "dead" interval brought about by repeated notes, when the repetition is from an accented to a weak one, is sometimes used to set off the closing modulation in certain types of fugue subjects.

However, pausing a bit after this rather technical digression into musical matters to look back at Jesus' fifth statement upon which the surrounding formal plan casts a light not unlike that of a spotlight focused on a character on stage, one becomes suddenly aware of the fact that this is the crucial utterance of the whole text:

Whosoever drinketh of this water that I shall give him shall never thirst;

(At this point the writer must confess to being just a little uneasy that the examination of the several parts of the form may sidetrack the reader from keeping constantly in mind the form of the passage as a whole. One of the hazards of formal analysis is that it becomes so easy to lose sight of the entire organism when its constituent parts are brought up for examination. When this happens, a real loss has been suffered.)

Turning now to the set of eight statements in the closing "octave"—that is ideas 25 - 32 in the whole form and (13) - (20) by Jesus—we come upon a relatively simple form closely resembling the diatonic octave. Jesus used this same formal concept in the sequential arrangement of the Beatitudes.

First, he "halved" the eight-idea form by using almost identical wordings in the first and fifth statements (i.e. Jesus' (13) and (17) ideas).

61

25. (13) Woman, believe me, the hour cometh, when ye shall neither in this mountain, nor yet at Jerusalem, worship the Father.
26. (14) Ye worship ye know not what:
27. (15) We know what we worship: for
28. (16) salvation is of the Jews.

---

29. (17) But the hour cometh, and now is, when the true worshippers shall worship the Father in spirit and in truth: for
30. (18) the Father seeketh such to worship him.
31. (19) God is a Spirit: and
32. (20) they that worship him must worship him in spirit and in truth.

(Perhaps we should have pointed out that Jesus' first six statements also were "halved"; the first three ideas being quite different and separated by means of four statements by the woman from the latter three.)

But, an effective application of the 5 : 3 division also exists here, and in the next chapter we shall encounter the same basic plan used somewhat differently in the woman's part of the dialogue.

The set of five statements at the beginning of this eight-idea segment, and the first of the closing three-idea group feature statements at important points that have many key words in common, as shown by those set apart in capital letters:

25. (13) Woman, believe me, the hour cometh, when ye shall neither in this mountain, nor yet at Jerusalem, WORSHIP THE FATHER.
26. (14) Ye worship ye know not what:
27. (15) we know what we worship: for
28. (16) salvation is of the Jews.
29. (17) But the hour cometh and now is, when the true worshippers shall WORSHIP THE FATHER in spirit and in truth: for
30. (18) THE FATHER seeketh such to WORSHIP him.

62

Thus, the formal significance of the three words, "worship the Father" (although juxtaposed in idea 30) can be seen graphically as in the following diagram.

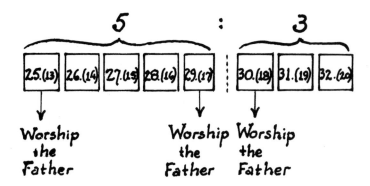

This brings into play two groups of ideas, each containing an uneven number of statements. In view of what takes place elsewhere in this conversation it is reasonable to expect that the central ideas of corresponding groups of this nature should have a special relationship to each other. And in the present eight-idea group they do!

In a so-called "real" fugue the "subject" (the thematic idea that serves as basis of the composition) on the third note of the scale (Mi) has as its "answer" the identical or corresponding idea on the seventh note of the scale (Ti). In the first group of five ideas the central statement is "we know what we worship" and the central idea of the closing group is "God is a spirit." By thinking of the preceding diagram in terms of the musical scale and the fugal relationship within it this eight-idea form can appear thus:

63

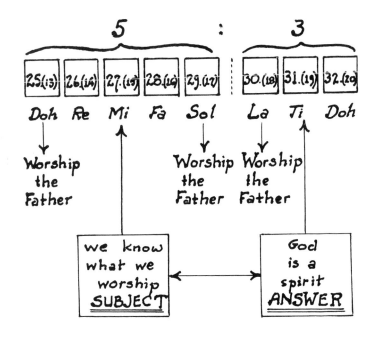

A curious and fascinating precedent for this fugal subject-answer relationship occurs in Psalm 1, which has a 13-idea form that corresponds in the minutest detail to the 13-note chromatic scale in which the Mi-Ti relationship occurs at the fifth and twelfth notes. In Psalm 1 the fifth idea says that the righteous man will "meditate" day and night, while in the twelfth idea it tells that the Lord "knoweth." And even in our day thoughtful and prudent people rarely, if ever, say that they "know." They are much more likely to say that they "have observed," they "are aware of," that "it appears to be," etc., etc. But, here Jesus speaking as Deity in no uncertain terms and without qualification says, "We *know* what we worship, (for) God *is* a spirit."

(The writer, studiously desiring to avoid taking any liberties with the Biblical text, is a bit concerned about those readers who may consider it too subjective to apply the fugal principle to literary ideas of this nature. However, after devoting much time and thought to the rarified atmosphere of theoretical counterpoint, the Subject-Answer principle—as the ultimate glorification of the God-given harmonic series—takes on an objectivity and penetration that extends into almost every phase of the creative process.)

The 5:3 (or as the retrograde of 3:5) ratio is an important proportion in every field of art. Paintings and mosaics in which figures are grouped in threes and fives as parts of a larger plan can readily be found. The eight-measure period in music is, of course, based upon this principle, but those periods that close with a final tonic chord are deceiving to the uninitiated because the 5:3 division is not visible until one becomes aware of the fact that the ending is brought about by moving the first one or two abstract measures to the end. This puts a significant 4th or 6th abstract measure at some other point—ostensibly—in the period. In its simplest usage, as encountered by a beginner in musical composition, this principle results in six eight-measure period forms as follows:

Group I, *having some conspicuous feature on sixth abstract measure* –

(a) Does not end:

(b) Ends with final I chord on 8th measure:

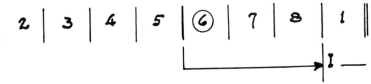

(c) Ends with final I chord beginning on 7th measure:

65

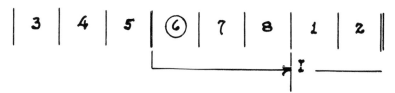

Group II, having some conspicuous feature on fourth abstract measure —

(a) Does not end:

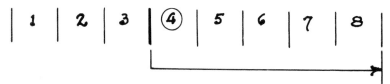

(b) Ends with final I chord on 8th measure:

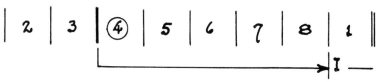

(c) Ends with final I chord beginning on 7th measure:

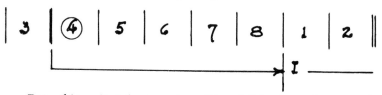

But, this principle is not readily visible from the printed music because in a period such as Group I (b), for example, the theoretical second measure that begins the period "looks" as though it were actually the first measure (which, insofar as practical effect is concerned, it is).

The general lack of awareness that all eight-measure periods, except those that do not end, have a double form plan has caused much misapprehension on the part of composition students. And, for some unexplainable reason, textbook writers show a chronic reluctance to mention the fact that all such periods have both a "visible and invisible" formal scheme.

Especially does this misapprehension become evident when unsuspecting students undertake to analyze the Bach chorales, or to harmonize assigned chorale melodies. One of the most common types of chorale lines is that in which there are seven notes preceding the terminal fermata. These are generally written so that the line begins on the fourth quarter in a measure and the fermata comes on the third quarter two measures later. Usually, such lines embody in quarter-note dimensions the form plans I (b) and II (b) either singly or in combination—the latter being the more common. This is one of Bach's greatest secrets that is rarely passed on to students. In a Bach chorale harmonization, the chords and discords are without exception subservient to the formal considerations.

Other examples of the 5:3 or 3:5 principle are legion in number and it would take volumes to deal fully with this one aspect of form. However, one more instance may be in order.

Every Sunday untold millions of worshippers "humbly confess" their "sins unto Almighty God" by means of the familiar *General Confession*. But, do they realize that they are confessing *five* things and ask in return *three* things to help them improve their unfortunate situation? In *The Book of Common Prayer* it appears in one paragraph thus, with no visible demonstration of the underlying proportion plan:

Almighty and most merciful Father; We have erred, and strayed from thy ways like lost sheep. We have followed too much the devices and desires of our own hearts. We have offended against thy holy laws. We have left undone those things which we ought to have done; And we have done those things which we ought not to have done; And there is no health in us. But thou, O Lord, have mercy upon us, miserable offenders. Spare thou those. O God, who confess their faults. Restore thou those who are penitent; According to thy promises declared unto mankind in Christ Jesus our Lord. And grant, O most merciful Father, for his sake; That we may hereafter live a godly, righteous, and sober life, To the glory of the holy Name. Amen.

But by writing out the *General Confession* in a tabular format, this ratio plan becomes crystal clear:

Almighty and most merciful Father;
(1) We have erred, and strayed from thy ways like lost sheep.
(2) We have followed too much the devices and desires of our own hearts.
(3) We have offended against thy holy laws.
(4) We have left undone those things which we ought to have done;
(5) And we have done those things which we ought not to have done;
       And there is no health in us.
But thou, O Lord, have mercy upon us, miserable offenders.
(1) Spare thou those, O God, who confess their faults.
(2) Restore thou those who are penitent; According to thy promises declared unto mankind In Christ Jesus our Lord.
(3) And grant, O most merciful Father, for his sake; That we may hereafter live a godly, righteous, and sober life,
       To the glory of thy holy Name. Amen.

The 5:3 form is disguised by two means. First, the entire Confession is cast in one paragraph, with no attempt at showing the division. And, secondly, the two sets of ideas are both preceded and followed by introductory and coda-like clauses or sentences.

As in the case of Jesus' eight-statement form in the closing thirteen-idea "octave" of his conversation with the woman of Samaria, so the two sections of the *General Confession* can be subdivided and re-evaluated, but this chore is being left to the reader.

At this point it will suffice to mention that while neither the composition student doing his homework, nor the devout worshipper penitently confessing his sins may be aware of it, both are exercising themselves in the same energy generating arithmetical form division principle.

Jesus' final statement—the 34th of the entire dialogue and his *ninth* within this closing thirteen-idea "octave"; namely,

"I that speak unto thee am he"—brings into play again the haunting number nine. And, those who enjoy speculating upon this number as the symbol of completion or perfection are at liberty to do so to any extent they wish; but, as has been said before, anything in the way of speculative interpretation is quite outside the scope of this little volume. Some more things, however, about this final single statement are being saved for a later chapter.

It has been shown how the 13 : 21 and 21 : 13 ratios function in this conversation in at least three. ways. Two of these come about in the formal division of the text, while the third—as previously mentioned—exists in the fact that in the whole dialogue Jesus contributes twenty-one statements and the woman thirteen. In this text, the systematic divisions of the twenty-one-section portions are not too obvious, but to provide a twenty-one-unit form that is built on the Dynamic Symmetry principle a poem by Walt Whitman may be quoted.

EIDÓLONS

1.

I met a seer,
Passing the hues and objects of the world,
The fields of art and learning, pleasure, sense,
To glean eidólons.

2.

Put in thy chants said he,
No more the puzzling hour nor day, nor segments, parts, put in,
Put first before the rest as light for all and entrance-song of all,
That of eidólons.

3.

Ever the dim beginning,
Ever the growth, the rounding of the circle,
Ever the summit and the merge at last, (to surely start again,)
Eidólons! eidólons!

69

4.

Ever the mutable,
Ever materials, changing, crumbling, re-cohering,
Ever the ateliers, the factories divine,
    Issuing eidólons.

5.

Lo, I or you,
Or woman, man, or state, known or unknown,
We seeming solid wealth, strength, beauty build,
    But really build eidólons.

6.

The ostent evanescent,
The substance of an artist's mood or savant's studies long,
Or warrior's, martyr's, hero's toils,
    To fashion his eidólon.

7.

Of every human life,
(The units gather'd, posted, not a thought, emotion, deed, left
        out,)
The whole or large or small summ'd, added up,
    In its eidólon.

8.

The old, old urge,
Based on the ancient pinnacles, lo, newer, higher pinnacles,
From science and the modern still impell'd,
    The old, old urge, eidólons.

9.

The present now and here,
America's busy, teeming, intricate whirl,
Of aggregate and segregate for only thence releasing,
    To-day's eidólons.

10.

These with the past,
Of vanish'd lands, of all the reigns of kings across the sea,
Old conquerors, old campaigns, old sailors' voyages,
Joining eidólons.

11.

Densities, growth, façades,
Strata of mountains, soils, rocks, giant trees,
Far-born, far-dying, living long, to leave,
Eidólons everlasting.

12.

Exalté, rapt, ecstatic,
The visible but their womb of birth,
Of orbic tendencies to shape and shape and shape,
The mighty earth-eidólon.

13.

All space, all time,
(The stars, the terrible perturbations of the suns,
Swelling, collapsing, ending, serving their longer, shorter use,)
Fill'd with eidólons only.

14.

The noiseless myriads,
The infinite oceans where the rivers empty,
The separate countless free identities, like eyesight,
The true realities, eidólons.

15.

Not this the world,
Nor these the universes, they the universes,
Purport and end, ever the permanent life of life,
Eidólons, eidólons.

16.

Beyond thy lectures learn'd professor,
Beyond thy telescope or spectroscope observer keen, beyond all
    mathematics.
Beyond the doctor's surgery, anatomy, beyond the chemist with
    his chemistry,
The entities of entities, eidólons.

17.

Unfix'd yet fix'd,
Ever shall be, ever have been and are,
Sweeping the present to the infinite future,
    Eidólons, eidólons, eidólons.

18.

The prophet and the bard,
Shall yet maintain themselves, in higher stages yet,
Shall mediate to the Modern, to Democracy, interpret yet to them,
    God and eidólons.

19.

And thee my soul,
Joys, ceaseless exercises, exaltations,
Thy yearning amply fed at last, prepared to meet,
    Thy mates, eidólons.

20.

Thy body permanent,
The body lurking there within thy body,
The only purport of the form thou art, the real I myself,
    An image, an eidólon.

21.

Thy very songs not in thy songs,
No special strains to sing, none for itself,
But from the whole resulting, rising at last and floating,
    A round full-orb'd eidólon.

Without stopping to go into a detailed analysis of Walt Whitman's poem, it will suffice to say that "America" is mentioned only once—in the ninth stanza, thereby beginning the larger segment of thirteen stanzas in contrast to the eight-stanza section at the beginning. In addition to the single mention of Whitman's beloved America, the 8 : 13 division is stressed by abrupt opposites in time: the eighth stanza deals with the "old, old," while the ninth stanza stresses "The present now and here."

The retrograde 13 : 8 division, although less forceful, is shown by a not dissimilar set of opposites. The thirteenth stanza speaks of "the terrible perturbations of the suns," which is immediately followed by "The noiseless myriads," in the fourteenth stanza.

When an art form in any medium is divided into the same proportion forwards and in retrograde, it is traditional practice to make the two division effects unequal in intensity. Thus, even in the divisions themselves, a kind of calculated proportion exists.

The reader may wish to spend a little more time with this Whitman poem in objective examination.

CHAPTER IX

As one turns to the woman's part in the conversation with Jesus, one cannot help but sense a kind of counterpoint between two personalities—a counterpoint as pregnant with thematic interplay as any exercise that a composer may write.

The beginner in counterpoint is given a cantus firmus against which he must write a counterpoint which moves according to a collection of rules and restrictions that are applied both vertically and melodically. To a great extent the success of such a counterpoint is determined by the amount of dissonance achieved within the framework of technical resources made available to him by the rules.

Contrary to common belief, dissonance and harshness are not synonymous. Rather, dissonance—as a technicality—is a situation that requires resolution to a concord. The outstanding example is the six-four chord which, although relatively mild in effect, is dissonant to the degree that it must "move on" to a point of resolution.

In the same sense any two people when conversing or working together form a kind of human counterpoint in which more or less discord is virtually inevitable. But, such discord is not necessarily unpleasant or harsh. In fact, in the realm of human relations many thoroughly pleasant situations require resolution to a point of finality as well as do the more disagreeable ones.

But, someone may ask, "In the conversation under examination, which speaker represents the *cantus firmus* and which the *counterpoint?*" These are the two energy generating forces. The obvious answer is that these functions, namely that of challenger and defender, alternate between the two participants, as is usually the case between the subject and countersubject of a fugue. And herein lies a problem that often baffles counterpoint students as they progress to the more advanced considerations of fugue: how the themes alternate, according to the composer's artistic desires, in the role of cantus firmus and opposing counterpoint. In general, the part that requires resolution at a given moment is the counterpoint, while the cantus firmus provides a sort of platform of stability.

Thus, if we can spare a moment to re-read the conversation it will be seen that—exactly as in musical counterpoint—Jesus and the woman alternately set up queries or demands that require "resolution." And the rhythm of this human "counterpoint" will be discussed in the next chapter, but first it is necessary to examine the forms of the woman's utterances in the two terminal thirteen-idea "octaves." In the first of these we find a form of eight statements that extends one unit beyond the thirteen-idea "octave" and dovetails into the middle section of the over-all form. This also brings into being the external form discussed in Chapter VI.

2. *(1) How is it that thou, being a Jew, askest drink of me, which am a woman of Samaria? for*

3. *(2) the Jews have no dealings with the Samaritans.*

6. *(3) Sir, thou hast nothing to draw with, and*

7. *(4) the well is deep:*

8. *(5) from whence then hast thou that living water?*

9. *(6) Art thou greater than our father Jacob, which*
      gave us the well,
      and drank thereof himself,
      and his children,
      and his cattle?

13. *(7) Sir, give me this water, that I thirst not,*

14. *(8) neither come hither to draw.*

Unlike Jesus' eight-statement form in the closing thirteen-idea "octave," this eight-idea form by the woman is not conspicuously cut in half. But, as in Jesus' eight-statement form, the Dynamic Symmetry division of 5:3 is present. The first section of five ideas is defined by question marks. And in the same way, the sixth statement that marks the beginning of the closing three-idea section is a question. Thus, in this eight-idea form by the woman, the question-mark serves the same purpose—insofar as the form goes—as the words "worship the Father" do in Jesus' form. Thus, we can make a double diagram:

WOMAN:

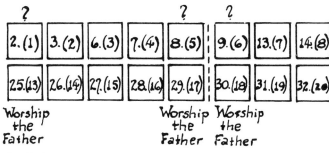

JESUS:

The woman's seventh idea, "Sir, give me this water," has been mentioned for its formal significance in an earlier chapter, and now comes into focus anew. Not only is this the fugal "answer" within the woman's first eight statements, but it is so situated that it also forms the terminal points of the first thirteen-idea "octave"; and thereby becomes a beautiful example of a multiple-purposed effect. How closely this resembles the art of orchestration when this great musical skill is applied creatively!

In the preceding chapter it was pointed out how in Jesus' eight-idea form the third and seventh idea brought into play the fugal subject-answer concept. In the woman's eight-idea form this same relationship appears, but—again—in a different way. Her third and seventh statements both begin with "Sir" and in addition show a reversal of awareness: "thou hast nothing to draw with" which is fugally answered by "give me this water." Thus, we can complete the above diagram, as shown on the next page:

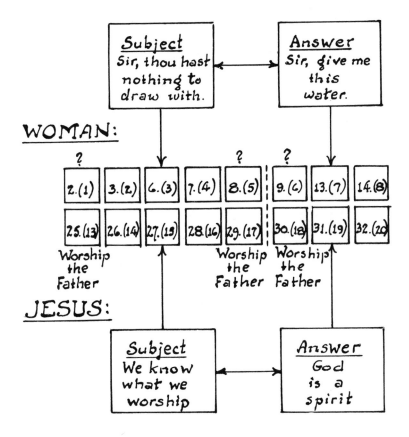

This is nothing new to skilled composers using as a matter of course a theme, characteristic harmonic progression, orchestral effect, or some other device to serve more than one purpose in defining a form. The Bach chorale harmonizations are full of such situations in the guise of chords, dissonances or significant voice-leadings. The use of multiple-purposed effects—in whatever art—is perhaps one of the best evidences of genuine technical skill and serious creative insight.

In the closing thirteen-idea "octave" the woman makes but four statements—a group of three concerning perception which

leads to the fourth statement on something that is to her of
supreme importance and which she knows all about:

22. *(10) Sir, I perceive that thou art a prophet.*
23. *(11) Our fathers worshipped in this mountain; and*
24. *(12) ye say, that in Jerusalem is the place where men ought
    to worship.*

---

33. *(13) I know that Messias cometh, which is called Christ:
    when he is come, he will tell us all things.*

Herewith is demonstrated what is at once one of the most
important and one of the most misunderstood aspects of rhythm;
since rhythm is really nothing more or less than form in very
small dimensions.

Most children are taught in their music lessons to "count
time" from bar line to bar line, thus:

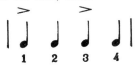

This is a gross misconception which many students never out-
grow! It is a vicious falsehood, perpetuated from generation to
generation by well-meaning people who never once suspect that
they are misinformed and that they are spreading their misconception amongst all with whom they come in contact. Yet, the
vast number of music students whose vision and musical sense
is throughout their entire lives thwarted and misdirected hereby
can never be counted.

And yet, if one will but observe, Third Species Counterpoint
shows the way and holds the secret to real rhythmical insight.
In this species all the rules are based upon the single truth
that a rhythm operates as follows from the second beat in any
given measure into the first beat in the subsequent measure,
thus:

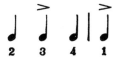

Most of the rules have one primary purpose: namely to make certain that this three-note "lead" from the second quarter of one measure into the first quarter of the subsequent measure maintains its direction unswervingly until it reaches its goal. And how many are the ways in which this "lead" can be shaped into a graceful and forceful arc of the purest melody!

And the accent on the third quarter of the measure middles this three-note "lead", and the counterpoint rules provide that this mid-point may be either a concord or discord depending upon the composer's intentions and the context with which he surrounds this central point of the "lead."

In a large measure grammar uses this same principle. Songwriters are aware of this more, perhaps, than anybody else. It is not often that one says anything that begins on an accent. For instance, the definite and indefinite articles, expletives, adjectives, etc., are all essentially rhythmic devices to set up an anacrusis. Just a few common phrases will illustrate:

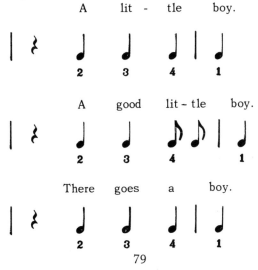

There goes a lit - tle boy.

2 3 4 1

Some day some educator will see that grammar is essentially a study in rhythm. When that day comes, grammar will no longer be a stilted and boresome thing, but will suddenly come alive and sparkle, and to many the use of language will take on a new and intriguing effectiveness.

Gilbert understood all this when he wrote his celebrated texts for Sullivan's music. Almost every line is a gem. The translators who produced the King James' version of the Psalms must have been aware of this wonderful aspect of language. And so were Lord Byron and Walt Whitman; and, of course, other poets worthy of the name.

Thus, the sequence of these four of the woman's statements—progressing as they do from ''I perceive'' to ''I know''—illustrate a simple, overpoweringly important and very deep principle. And this principle could be taught to every child through many diffrent subjects if teachers only sensed this wonderful thing! In fact, this is the basic principle behind the three bases leading to the home plate in baseball.

The ultimate demonstration of this principle is in the birth of a child. The nine month span comprises three thirteen week periods—or more colorfully, three seasons—and at the beginning of the fourth season the child is born. It is literally true that ''Life Begins at Forty''—at the fortieth week preceded by three thirteen-week rhythmical units.

By the same token and according to the same rhythmic plan, the woman progresses from ''I perceive'' to ''I know''—a veritable rebirth indeed!

CHAPTER X

In counterpoint the cantus firmus is one self-contained entity, the counterpoint another entity complete in itself and the union of the cantus firmus with the counterpoint makes for a third entity. From this point of view, then, we must approach the conversation between Jesus and the Samaritan woman. The internal forms which we have isolated in the two preceding chapters must now be examined as they work together—mesh as it were—like gears to set in motion a gigantic sonata-allegro form of ideas. And, as in the highly systematic sonata-allegro form, every cohesive device is used: repetitions, divisions into sections, abrupt introduction of new material, and so on.

Let us look at the first thirteen-ideas first as a unit.

JESUS: 1. (1) Give me to drink.

WOMAN: 2. *(1) How is it that thou, being a Jew, askest drink of. me, which am a woman of Samaria? for*

3. *(2) the Jews have no dealings with the Samaritans.*

JESUS: 4. (2) If thou knewest the gift of God, and who it is that saith to thee, Give me to drink; thou wouldest have asked of him, and

5. (3) he would have given thee living water.

WOMAN: 6. *(3) Sir, thou hast nothing to draw with, and*

7. *(4) the well is deep:*

8. *(5) from whence then hast thou that living water?*

9. *(6) Art thou greater than our father Jacob, which gave us the well,*
and drank thereof himself,
and his children,
and his cattle?

JESUS: 10. (4) Whosoever drinketh of this water shall thirst again: But

11. (5) whosoever drinketh of the water that I shall give him shall never thirst; but

12. (6) the water that I shall give him shall be in him a well of water springing up into everlasting life.

WOMAN: 13. *(7) Sir, give me this water, that I thirst not,*

The first conspicuous division occurs between the eighth and ninth ideas, thereby setting in motion the 8 : 5 relationship. The section of five ideas that forms the second part of the 13-idea "octave" begins with a question about "our father Jacob" quite unlike anything else in the entire dialogue.

First, it changes the subject completly and abruptly. Secondly, it is a complicated statement with a fourpoint thumbnail biography of Jacob and history of the well. Finally, it is another multiple-function idea in that, as was pointed out in the preceding chapter, it divides the woman's first eight ideas into the 5 : 3 ratio. Likewise it divides the opening thirteen-idea "octave" of the whole form into 8 : 5. And the wonder of all this is that the two forms thus marked off by this single idea neither begin nor end at the same time. What an idea for use in a symphony! What absolutely incredible craftsmanship in the distribution and utilization of ideas!

Next let us turn to the first segment of eight ideas leading up to this noteworthy ninth idea (and here this persistent "nine" rears its head again). Within this eight-idea form wonder upon wonder confronts us. First it consists of three ideas by Jesus and five by the woman. Here is our first 3 : 5 ratio. Of these, Jesus' statements come in the arrangement of 1 : 2, and the woman's in the arrangement of 2 : 4, which is, of course, nothing but 1 : 2 doubled. But, the 5 : 3 division of the eight ideas as a form is even more ingenious.

In the fifth statement, closing the first five-idea segment, Jesus says, "he would have given thee *living water*." In the eighth idea, the woman answers, "from whence then hast thou that *living water*?" Thus, the phrase "living water," used nowhere else in the entire conversation, closes the two sections of this eight-idea form.

But, still this is not all: when Jesus says "living water" it comes in his third statement, and when the woman repeats this phrase in her fifth statement, another 3:5 balance occurs. It is as though the reporter of the conversation was possessed with the thought of presenting the material so that no possible exercise of formal ingenuity would be overlooked.

The closing group of five statements in this opening thirteen-idea "octave" is, on a smaller scale, no less ingenious. The first and most obvious observation is that it consists of three statements of Jesus flanked by two of the woman:

WOMAN: 9. *(6) Art thou greater than our father Jacob, which gave us the well,*
and drank thereof himself,
and his children,
and his cattle?

JESUS: 10. (4) Whosoever drinketh of this water shall thirst again: But

11. (5) whosoever drinketh of the water that I shall give him shall never thirst; but

12. (6) the water that I shall give him shall be in him a well of water springing up into everlasting life.

WOMAN: 13. *(7) Sir, give me this water, that I thirst not,*

But there is a more subtle use of the 2:3 ratio. Two statements, 9 and 10, concern Jacob's well and the water therefrom while the remaining three—11, 12 and 13—are about Jesus' "living water" although this expression is not used verbatim within this set of five ideas. The 1:2 and 2:1 ratios within these three statements by Jesus—i.e. 10, 11 and 12—were discussed in considerable detail two chapters earlier and need not receive further attention at this time.

Turning to the closing thirteen-idea "octave," we find

83

considerably less complexity than we encountered in the corresponding "octave" at the beginning that has just been examined. We are first of all struck by a straightforward eight-idea form (ideas 22-29) beginning with three statements by the woman and closing with five by Jesus culminating with the oft-quoted lines, "But the hour cometh, and now is, when the true worshippers shall worship the Father in spirit and in truth."

WOMAN: 22. *(10) Sir, I perceive that thou art a prophet.*
23. *(11) Our fathers worshipped in this mountain; and*
24. *(12) ye say, that in Jerusalem is the place where men ought to worship.*
JESUS: 25. (13) Woman, believe me, the hour cometh, when ye shall neither in this mountain, not yet at Jerusalem, worship the Father.
26. (14) Ye worship ye know not what:
27. (15) we know what we worship: for
28. (16) salvation is of the Jews.
29. (17) But the hour cometh, and now is, when the true worshippers shall worship the Father in spirit and in truth:

In rather a fascinating way the "dead interval" bringing into play the 3:5 ratio within these eight ideas is set up: it comes about by the repetition of the word Jerusalem. In the third idea of this segment of eight, the woman says to Jesus, "ye say, that in Jerusalem is the place where man ought to worship." But, Jesus had said no such thing, at least not as the conversation is recorded in St. John's Gospel. According to the Biblical account, he had just met the woman at the well and, from the implications of the account as given, she did not recognize him. Thus, it would seem that this confrontation on her part could not possibly indicate any general policy on Jesus' part outside of this conversation.

Curiously enough, Jesus does not deny having said this, but instead takes "Jerusalem" as a starting point for a quite lengthy discourse on the nature of worship. As was pointed out in the case of other repetitions, this mention of Jerusalem—

84

irrelevant as a part of the dialogue—is to all appearances an extraneous element brought in to show a division point.

The closing five statements—30 - 34—are likewise exceedingly simple in their Dynamic Symmetry set-up. There are, quite naively, merely three statements elaborating further on the general theme of worship and two concerning the Messias. Of these two, one is by the woman and the other by Jesus.

JESUS: 30. (18) the Father seeketh such to worship him.

31. (19) God is a Spirit: and

32. (20) they that worship him must worship him in spirit and in truth.

WOMAN: 33. *(13) I know that Messias cometh, which is called Christ: when he is come, he will tell us all things.*

JESUS: 34. (21) I that speak unto thee am he.

From the foregoing it will be seen how the two characters weave a counterpoint that makes two balancing thirteen-idea terminal "octaves," within which and between which a multiplicity of formal relationships operate simultaneously—veritably a demonstration of the familiar "wheels within wheels" principle.

But, it is interesting to note that in a still more subtle way these two terminal forms are *not* equal in complexity. Thus, we encounter a new approach to Dynamic Symmetry which cannot be expressed in exact numerical terms.

In his book, *God's Reach,* Glenn Clark points out that Jesus gave his parables in pairs with one of the parables being both longer and more intense than the other. The first chapter of Genesis tells about the two lights—one greater than the other.

But this all points to a common problem in human relations. The soloist is naturally more colorful and predominating than his accompanist. In opera the orchestra is subordinate to the singing and acting on the stage, for the most part.

In the visual arts one color predominates while the accompanying colors are subordinate to it, or are derivative of it. In the news of the day one story of overpowering appeal is given more prominence than the others. In an athletic or oratorical contest, the winner is greater than the loser. And so on into whatever realm of endeavor one cares to look.

At this point we can well afford to stress the fact that most Dynamic Symmetry in life cannot be expressed in terms of definite numbers. Most of the noblest relationships are based on the principle that in the meeting of any two minds one must have respect to the other in a perspective of relative greatness. Love must be reciprocal but in relative intensity. "An eye for an eye and a tooth for a tooth" then becomes truly obsolete.

For those with an inclination towards symbolic interpretation, this dialogue between the woman and Jesus—two unequal characters—in a design of marvelous complexity may gain additional meaning through an awareness of form: the silent language.

CHAPTER XI

When Percy Buck wrote his much used treatise, *Unfigured Harmony*, as a guide for British degree candidates in music, he treated the business of melody harmonization in a group of three chapters. These deal with the *beginning*, the *ending*, and the *middle* of a melody respectively.

As suggested earlier, the middle of any art form is an important matter that requires the most expert treatment. How many young composers have "lost their way" in the development section of a Sonata-allegro form? How many counterpoint students have become hopelessly enmeshed in needless complexities in the middle stretto entries of a fugue? And, how many college professors and preachers have learned to their sorrow that if a lecture or sermon "sags" in the middle it is well-nigh impossible ever to recapture the listener's attention once it has strayed away?

Thus, after having considered in some detail the form of the two end portions of the conversation between Jesus and the Samaritan woman, we come at length to the middle segment of eight ideas. This is not as well-defined a section as some of the others that have been discussed.

WOMAN: 14. *(8) neither come hither to draw.*

JESUS: 15. (7) Go, call thy husband, and
          16. (8) come hither.

WOMAN: 17. *(9) I have no husband.*

JESUS: 18. (9) Thou hast well said, I have no husband: for
          19.(10) thou hast had five husbands; and
          20.(11) he whom thou now hast is not thy husband:
          21.(12) in that saidst thou truly.

Here the Dynamic Symmetry centers on the word "husband," or "husbands," which appears in five of the eight ideas. This sets up a simple 3:5 ratio insomuch as five ideas feature the word "husband" and three do not. It was pointed out in an earlier chapter how the sentence, "I have no husband," was first stated by the woman and then quoted by Jesus to flank the middle of the entire form.

But more than this, the five appearances of "husband" are so arranged that they involve a span of six ideas—three on either side of the middle. Could it be that the statement without "husband" represents the current gentleman who, according to Jesus' blunt accusation, was *not* her husband?

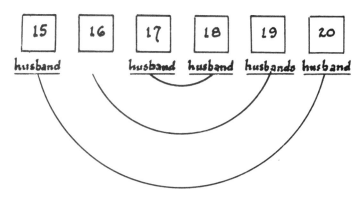

The Dynamic Symmetry within these five occurrences of "husband" is most ingenious. They can be tabulated as follows:

2	:	3
in		not in
quoted sentence		quoted sentence
(17, 18)		(15, 19, 20)

1	:	2
alone		contiguously
(15)		(19, 20)

1	:	2
plural		singular
(19)		(15, 20)

Taking the story by itself, apart from any formal considerations, the injection of the business of husbands seems irrelevant. The husbands—even the non-existent sixth one—have really nothing whatever to do with the ongoing discussion about water, and they seem not to be the basis for censure or for any sort of discourse on morality or fidelity.

But, when viewed on the basis of the development section of a sonata-allegro form, and especially so according to the requirements of progressive composers of the present day, the introduction of new and seemingly irrelevant material to lead on to the recapitulation offers a fresh approach to the problem, which might well be one of the most difficult that besets a young composer. Of course, this is done to some extent by every imaginative composer, but to build a whole development out of radically new and unrelated material is something else again and calls for creative insight of the highest order.

But, in another sense this business about the "husband" and the curious way in which it operates according to Dynamic Symmetry is important. It sets off the second part of the external veneer form mentioned in an earlier chapter. Thus, as so often happens in a musical composition, what at first appears to be an irrelevant and insignificant trifle turns out to be the unifying force of the whole systematic structure.

Anyone familiar with numbers in the symbolic sense knows that six has many unusual qualities not shared by other numbers, and just by leafing through a Bible concordance one can see at a glance how often this number enters into significant situations. And, very often a hexad of ideas operates at the very core of a form, sometimes so smoothly as to be almost imperceptible. Such a case exists in *The Book of Common Prayer* in *A General Thanksgiving*, the one prayer that "may be said by the Congregation with the Minister" both in the Morning and Evening Prayer. In the middle of this quite long prayer the members of the Congregation "bless" God for a list of six benefits. The sentence can be quoted in columnated form as follows:

"We bless thee for
(1) our creation,
(2) preservation, and
(3) all the blessings of this life; but above all, for
(4) thine inestimable love in the redemption of the world
by our Lord Jesus Christ; for
(5) the means of grace, and for
(6) the hope of glory."

However, in artistic construction six is often not employed in this way, but may be more generally found as 6 + 1 (as in the creation story which tells of six days of work plus one of rest) or as 6 - 1, as in the present instance where a six-idea section about "husband" has one statement with the key word not present.

Six, as a field for discovery, is virtually unlimited in every sphere of artistic structural endeavor and can provide the reader with endless diversion. More need not be said about it at this time.

This intrusion of "husband" into the conversation coupled with an interesting use of the imperative sentence on Jesus' part sets off the two divisions of the external veneer form. This division is brought about by his first and seventh statements (the 1st and 15th of the whole form), both of which are commands:

1. (1) Give me to drink.

and

15. (7) Go, call thy husband,

This second command is connected to another one—the significant second unit in the central six-idea "husband" form—"Go call thy husband, and come hither." Here a new and quite subtle approach to the Dynamic Symmetry relationship comes into play. Jesus utters two commands: a single one at the beginning and a double one at the inception of the second external portion of the form. Thus is brought about a situation where three becomes two, or in other words two consists of three.

Against these two imperative sentences by Jesus we find one by the woman, in her seventh statement, the thirteenth in the whole form.

13. *(7) Sir, give me this water,*

Again, a 1 : 2 ratio comes about: one imperative sentence by the woman and two by Jesus.

A curious technique comes into play at this point. Just as Jesus' seventh and eighth ideas merge to make one, so do the woman's seventh and eighth ideas combine and become one. It is still more fascinating that in this merging process of two pairs of seven and eight being merged to form two ones, the eighth idea of Jesus quotes the "come hither" from the eighth idea of the woman:

WOMAN: 13. *(7) Sir, give me this water, that I thirst not,*

          14. *(8) neither come hither to draw.*

JESUS: 15. (7) Go, call thy husband, and

        16. (8) come hither.

In the marriage ceremony two become one, but the one is the third entity—that is, the family itself. Thus, the two people involved bring about three situations: (1) the husband alone, (2) the wife alone and (3) the husband and wife together—this union being the productive mechanism for the continuation of life on this earth.

On the basis of what has been shown above, the entrance of the "husband" hexad into the core of the conversation causes form: the silent language to demonstrate a principle to anyone who will avail himself of its significance, and has the opportunity and imagination to put it into operation.

CHAPTER XII

An interesting facet of serious thought is that any artistic and formal crystallization brings into being—both within and outside of itself—by-products quite frequently neither intended nor envisioned by the artist. It is not unusual to find that a thoroughly thought-out work of art is considerably more ingenious than the artist had ever meant it to be. In fact, it is not unusual for an artist to be quite amazed by what somebody else might see or hear in his work.

This brings us afresh to the wonders of counterpoint, as presented in the five academic species. No field of learning within the arts is more generally misunderstood and more vociferously belittled. But for those capable of reading beneath the surface the counterpoint species cast a never flickering light that illuminates every corner of the whole realm of musical achievement—whether in the field of composing or in the realm of performance. The five species constitute a norm, both melodically and harmonically, from which everyone is free to deviate to whatever extent his artistic needs and inclinations require.

But, getting back to the matter of by-products of serious thought more specifically, we can find an especially interesting example in the art of writing fugue subjects so that they will produce certain predetermined stretto formations. Suppose that as an adventure in theoretical counterpoint a composer set himself a problem in fugue as follows:

Compose a five-measure tonal subject beginning on the III and closing on the V that will produce three different stretti as follows:

(a) at the 5th above at one measure
(b) at the 8th below at one measure
(c) at the 4th below at two measures

The problem is a relatively simple one in a specific canonic application of double counterpoint. But, what will fascinate the composer once he has solved the problem to his musical satisfaction is that the subject evolving from this exercise will invariably produce several other stretto formations in addition to those stipulated in the given problem. In fact, many of these by-product stretti may be better musically, especially as concerns harmonization, than the ones originally intended.

But, then, another problem arises. A composer will be able to recognize and use these by-product stretti only to the degree in which he is alert to the stretto possibilities within the twelve categories in which a stretto can operate:

1. Literal
2. Retrograde
3. Contrary Motion
4. Augmentation
5. Diminution
6. Retrograde & Contrary Motion
7. Retrograde & Augmentation
8. Retrograde & Diminution
9. Contrary Motion & Augmentation
10. Contrary Motion & Diminution
11. Retrograde & Contrary Motion & Augmentation
12. Retrograde & Contrary Motion & Diminution

To the composer who is unaware of this sphere of stretto operation and its inherent possibilities—musically and technically—the above means absolutely nothing, and it is of not the slightest help to him.

Thus, we come to an attribute of form that is to some degree subjective—but in an intellectual sense, not an emotional one. Granting that the form in question is the product of serious thought on the part of the builder, it is safe to assume that it will contain far more than the creator of it intended. But, how is one to know where the artist's conscious planning leaves off and the by-products begin? Frankly, the writer does not have the temerity to propose an answer to this problem.

This question invariably arises when the rhythmic intricacies of a Bach Chorale harmonization, the carefully timed imitative entrances of a Palestrina Mass, the time ratios of a Beethoven sonata-allegro movement, or the subtleties of Tchaikovsky's orchestration are pointed out to a class of students. Someone will ask, "But did the composer actually plan all this?" or "Did the composer know he was doing so many interesting things?" Who knows?

In this spirit, tinged perhaps with intellectual and objective subjectivity (if such a seemingly contradictory term is possible), let us look again at the conversation between Jesus and the Samaritan woman and take notice of a few formal intricacies that may—or may not—be by-products of the original planning. We shall dwell on just a few, and leave it to the reader to speculate further in this direction if he so desires.

Form is achieved through the definition of proportions. There is no other way. And in the more subtle forms, proportions are defined in two general ways:

(1) by the recurrence—either literally or in variation—of significant motives or ideas,

and

(2) by the introduction of material different from that of the context.

In earlier chapters we have seen these two principles exemplified through the repetition of key phrases such as "Give me to drink," and "living water," and "I have no husband"; and through the introduction of new and seemingly irrelevant material such as "husband" for the first time in the 15th unit of the 34-idea form.

In connection herewith it was shown how the middle of the form was flanked in ideas seventeen and eighteen by the simple declarative sentence, "I have no husband"; and how this was in each case the ninth statement by both the woman and Jesus. This sets off two equally balanced halves of seventeen ideas each.

Now, the mid-point of a seventeen-idea form—which is what each half turns out to be—is again the ninth idea in each set. In the first half this would be statement number nine and in

94

the latter half number twenty-six. Do these two statements have a connection? They certainly appear to combine in meaning, but this is perhaps so firmly within the realm of subjective interpretation that it may be wiser to let the reader decide for himself. At any rate here they are:

WOMAN: 9. *(6) Art thou greater than our father Jacob, which gave us the well, and drank thereof himself, and his children, and his cattle?*

JESUS: 26. (14) Ye worship ye know not what:

If we can accept Jesus' fourteenth statement as a reply to the question in the woman's ninth statement this would put Jesus on record as having spoken disparagingly and bluntly against the Samaritan religion in which much was made of Jacob's well and of the mountain at the foot of which the well is found.

Looking for a corresponding pair of such superimposed relationships, we find the woman addressing Jesus as "Sir" three times, in ideas six, thirteen and twenty-two thereby marking off another seventeen-unit segment within the whole form. The middle, or ninth idea of this seventeen-unit segment is the woman's eighth idea, "neither come hither to draw."

Again, in the ninth idea of the whole form—the woman's sixth idea—the extraneous character "Jacob" is introduced. Corresponding with this is the introduction of the equally irrelevant "Jerusalem" in ideas twenty-four and twenty-five. Thus another seventeen-idea segment is blocked off within the form from Jacob to the second mention of Jerusalem, ideas 9-25 the middle idea of which is the woman's ninth statement, "I have no husband." Now, if we combine these two mid-point statements and let them be preceded by the woman's seventh (or second "Sir") idea we get the following very simple reason why the woman would like nothing better than to be relieved of the drudgery of fetching water:

13. *(7) Sir, give me this water, that I thirst not,*
14. *(8) neither come hither to draw.*
17. *(9) I have no husband.*

95

The implications are too elementary to be by-passed. The poor soul was sick and tired of coming to carry water, and she had no husband to help her with the wearisome chore; and herein we find the simplest sort of everyday human problem. But, one may ask, is it correct and right to derive sequences of literary ideas by this method? Is not a piece of writing simply to be read "right through?" And cannot totally erroneous meanings be manufactured by this process?

Ordinarily, the doubts expressed in the preceding paragraph are justified; and this process of reading thoughts out of the normal sequence can be a dangerous one, but in the case of an unusually well conceived form the key points will under certain conditions render new and interesting meanings.

In some of the pre-Bach German choral harmonizations key points are often found to produce a superimposed tonality quite apart from that in which the chorale as a whole is cast. And in Bach's twenty-one section organ Passacaglia in C minor an analysis of the rhythmic texture of the variations will show that exactly as there are in the conversation between Jesus and the Samaritan woman two pairs of seventeen-idea segments, so are there two pairs of eleven-section variation forms brought into play by the combination of textural techniques and characteristic manipulations of the ground bass. And as in the conversation, two of the seventeen-idea sections are placed end to end and the other two function concurrently just *away* from the center of the form, so in the Bach Passacaglia do the four eleven-section superimpositions operate.

Before leaving this matter of observing word repetitions and similar devices that might either have come about through being "planted" or as a by-product, let us examine just one more.

Three mentions are made of "Jew"—twice by the woman and once by Jesus, thereby bringing in a $1:2$ relationship in retrograde. Moreover, it is used twice in the plural and once in the singular; again a $1:2$ situation. In addition, it is used once in the plural by both the woman and Jesus, thus effecting the ever-important $1:1$ preliminary ratio.

But, these three statements lifted out of context throw into sharp relief an assertion by Jesus that may pose a theological problem for many Christians.

WOMAN: 2. *(1) How is it that thou, being a Jew, askest drink of me, which am a woman of Samaria? for*
3. *(2) the Jews have no dealings with the Samaritans.*

JESUS: 28. (16) salvation is of the Jews.

It is fascinating to contemplate how a Christian clergyman might build a sermon around Jesus' statement that "salvation is of the Jews." And, if we read the whole sentence in which this clause appears, it will be noted that this statement is not distorted or misrepresented by being read or considered alone. In fact, the whole sentence, comprising ideas 26 - 28 of the whole form, builds up to this surprising assertion. Jesus told the Samaritan woman in no uncertain terms:

"Ye worship ye know not what: we know what we worship: *for salvation is of the Jews.*"

Now, refer back to the quotation from the form given two paragraphs earlier and note how the recognition of the recurrence of "Jew" together with the Dynamic Symmetry conditions involved throws, as it were, a spotlight on the clause, "salvation is of the Jews."

Does this bring about a theological misrepresentation, or does it point up an important truth not ordinarily recognized or comprehended? Again, this is something that the reader must decide for himself; it is merely pointed out here that such a possibility exists.

So, in musical composition when figures or instrumental effects recur at seemingly strange places and in apparently irrelevant contexts, do they come about as a by-product or as a creative intention? Did Dürer offer a clue to this sort of thing in the clever diagram shown and dissected in Chapter IV?

Or, putting the question in another way, does form: the silent language, have a way of producing a kind of overtone all its own?

97

CHAPTER XIII

One hears it said at times that the whole is not greater than the sum of its parts. This may be true in some quarters, but it is an out-and-out fallacy in any product resulting from the creative principle of division, especially as manifested through Dynamic Symmetry. In the realm of ideas—regardless of the medium in which these ideas may be expressed—the whole is infinitely greater than the sum of its parts!

A dismantled violin—even with all of its parts present and in perfect condition—cannot sing a note. An automobile with even one essential part disconnected will not run. And an orchestra with its four choirs separated can play no symphony. Totality—which results in an operative mechanism—is, in fact, a truly wonderful thing.

We are constantly reminded of it, and yet—somehow—we forget it, chiefly because totality is difficult to grasp. Paul asserts that we are all members of "one body in Christ, and every one members one of another." And, in contrast, we see strange sects and cults whose theology is based on one small point in Scripture. Kant, in his characteristic way, says that the sum total of several experiences is not in itself an experience.

The danger of missing a whole because of the fascination of its parts is an ever-present one. The danger is right here in this little book, as it is in every other book—including the Bible itself. The little conversation between travel-weary Jesus and the Samaritan woman who was thoroughly "fed up" with the necessity of fetching water could have taken at most only a few minutes. In this little thirty-four statement chat between two tired people who chanced to meet at a public well under the not noon-day sun we find a veritable network of ideas arranged with incredible ingenuity according to the ageless principle of Dynamic Symmetry.

We isolated some of these parts, examined them and compared their formal arrangement with identical forms in other realms of activity. All this has been intriguing—at least to the writer. And, we have, perhaps, developed a feeling of awe as to the formal wonders of the holy Scriptures.

But we quite easily could have lost sight of the form as a whole and the impact created by the smaller internal forms all operating concurrently. A musician could well become so interested in the ingenuity displayed in the separate sections of the Bach organ Passacaglia in C minor that he would never quite sense the cumulative effect of the entire twenty-one section form in operation. A conscientious student could practice faithfully and thoughtfully a Beethoven sonata and be so concerned with the separate themes, inner voices, transitions, developments, etc., that the design of the wonderful sonata-allegro as a whole may quite elude him, as well as the audience for which he would play it.

The problem of totality is constantly before us. It is expressed generally in two ways—positively by "all" and negatively by "no." Consider for a moment the impact of the italicized words in the following quotation from Psalm 33, verses 13-16:

"The Lord looketh down from heaven, he beholdeth *all* the sons of men.

"From the place of his habitation he looketh upon *all* the inhabitants of the earth.

"He fashioneth their hearts alike; he considereth *all* their works.

"There is *no* king saved by the multitude of an host; etc."

Every Sunday morning for centuries untold millions of pious and penitent people recite the *General Confession* and, after having listed the five general ways in which they have sinned, they interject a sort of summary by saying, "And there is *no* health in us." But, in saying the "no" do they honestly mean that *everything* in their lives is wrong? Or, do they intend to imply that because some things are wrong there is no totality?

99

Or, can it be that some fail entirely to catch the implications of the "no"?

A curious parallel exists in the field of academic harmony. Although four-part harmony consists actually of six two-part combinations—Bass-Tenor, Bass-Alto, Bass-Soprano, Tenor-Alto, Tenor-Soprano and Alto-Soprano—an error in one of these two-part combinations brands the entire progression as incorrect. In the strictest thinking, the following progression is only one-sixth incorrect since the consecutive fifths come between Tenor and Alto. But, because of this one-sixth incorrectness, the entire progression must be, and generally is, considered as wholly imperfect.

Thus to conclude this study of the conversation between Jesus and the Samaritan woman we shall simply give the text again as it stands in the fourth chapter of St. John's Gospel and summarize our observations in two diagrams.

[1001]   **CHAPTER 4**

Jesus Talks with a Woman of Samaria

WHEN therefore the Lord knew how the Pharisees had heard that Jesus made and baptized more disciples than John,

CHAP. 4
a Gen. 33: 19
Gen. 48: 22
Josh. 24: 32

2 (Though Jesus himself baptized not, but his disciples,)

3 He left Judæa, and departed again into Galilee.

4 And he must needs go through Să-mā'rĭ-ā.

5 Then cometh he to a city of Să-mā'rĭ-ā, which is called Sȳ'-

chär, near to the parcel of ground *that Jacob gave to his son Joseph.

6 Now Jacob's well was there. Jesus therefore, being wearied with *his* journey, sat thus on the well: *and* it was about the sixth hour.

7 There cometh a woman of Să-mā′rĭ-ă to draw water: Jesus saith unto her, Give me to drink.

8 (For his disciples were gone away unto the city to buy meat.)

9 Then saith the woman of Să-mā′rĭ-ă unto him, How is it that thou, being a Jew, askest drink of me, which am a woman of Să-mā′rĭ-ă? for *the Jews have no dealings with the Samaritans.

10 Jesus answered and said unto her, If thou knewest *the gift of God, and who it is that saith to thee, Give me to drink; thou wouldest have asked of him, and he would have given thee *living water.

11 The woman saith unto him, Sir, thou hast nothing to draw with, and the well is deep: from whence then hast thou that living water?

12 Art thou greater than our father Jacob, which gave us the well, and drank thereof himself, and his children, and his cattle?

13 Jesus answered and said unto her, Whosoever drinketh of this water shall thirst again:

14 But *whosoever drinketh of the water that I shall give him shall never thirst; but the water that I shall give him *shall be in him a well of water springing up into everlasting life.

15 The *woman saith unto him, Sir, give me this water, that I thirst not, neither come hither to draw.

16 Jesus saith unto her, Go, call thy husband, and come hither.

17 The woman answered and said, I have no husband. Jesus said unto her, Thou hast well said, I have no husband:

18 For thou hast had five husbands; and he whom thou now hast is not thy husband: in that saidst thou truly.

19 The woman saith unto him, Sir, *I perceive that thou art a prophet.

20 Our fathers worshipped *in this mountain; and ye say, that in *Jerusalem is the place where men ought to worship.

21 Jesus saith unto her, Woman, believe me, the hour cometh, when *ye shall neither in this mountain, nor yet at Jerusalem, worship the Father.

22 Ye worship *ye know not what: we know what we worship: for *salvation is of the Jews.

. 23 But the hour cometh, and now is, when the true worshippers shall worship the Father in *spirit and in *truth: for the Father seeketh such to worship him.

24 God *is a Spirit: and they that worship him must worship *him* in spirit and in truth.

25 The woman saith unto him, I know that *Mĕs-sī′as cometh, which is called Christ: when he is come, he will tell us all things.

26 Jesus saith unto her, *I that speak unto thee am *he.*

A. D. 30
CHAP. 4
g Rom.6: 23 1 John 5: 20
h Luke 7: 16
i Gen. 12:6 Judg. 9:7
f Deut. 12: 5 2 Chr. 7: 12
k Mal. 1:11 1 Tim. 2: 8
l 2 Kin. 17:29
m Is. 2:3 Luke 24: 47 Rom. 9:4, 5
n ch. 14:17 Rom. 8:4 1 Cor. 3: 16 1 Cor. 6: 17 Gal. 5:25 Phil. 3:3
o ch. 1:17
p Acts 17: 24-29 2 Cor. 3: 17
q Deut. 18: 15 Dan. 9:24
r Mark 14: 61 ch. 9:37 ch. 10:36
s Job 23:12 ch. 6:38 ch. 17:4 ch. 19:30
t Matt. 9: 37 Luke 10: 2
u Ps. 19:11 Ps. 58:11 Prov. 11: 18 Dan. 12: 3 1 Cor. 3:8 James 5: 20 2 John 8
v Acts 10: 43 1 Pet. 1: 12
w Gen. 49:

Our first diagram concerns the characters in this little scene, and therein we find again a set of Dynamic Symmetry ratios in motion. There are three earthly characters—*two of* whom are present and *one* that is not. They are, of course, Jesus, the Jew, and the woman, a Samaritan. The missing character is the "husband," or the man currently associated with the woman. Then there are two characters referred to but not of this life—Jacob to whom the woman refers as "father" and God whom Jesus calls "Father." Thus we have a total of five personalities—three of this world and two of another realm.

Jesus and the woman both bring into the discussion two parallel lines of topics. Jesus talks about "living water" and worshipping the Father "in spirit and truth"; while the woman mentions "this water" from the well and Jacob "our father." These two lines of conversation on two different planes of thought and insight merge and culminate in the two closing ideas of the thirty-four statement form in which the woman begins to perceive the Messias, and Jesus acknowledges in complete frankness that the Messias is He. The following diagram in the shape of an arrowhead will illustrate this over-all direction of the form. (see next page.)

Our second diagram is merely a visual composite of all of the form mechanisms discussed in the preceding chapters. These now merge into one unified whole as the full text is read. The power created by the concurrent operation of these forms is something that becomes felt rather than seen or understood intellectually. (see end leaf at back of book.)

The same is true of a musical composition. People who know nothing of the intricate workings of a sonata-allegro form feel the impact of a Beethoven symphony. The confluence of form superimposed on form and relationship superimposed on relationship creates a sort of counterpoint whose impact is inevitable and inescapable.

The same is true in many aspects in the field of theoretical counterpoint. Many a student subjected to the canon technique complains long and loud that a so-called "crab" canon (that is, a canon in which one of the voices moves in retrograde) never can be heard as such because nobody listens to music in retro-

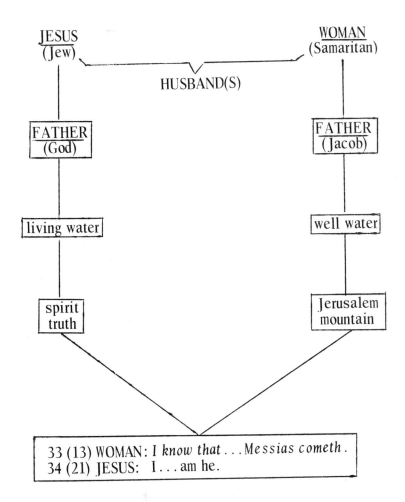

grade; and the more especially so if it becomes imbedded in a contrapuntal or harmonic texture. But that is not in any sense the issue. The order of harmonies initiated by such a canon builds up a kind of harmonic unity and logic of progression attainable in no other way. As much can be said for various applications of double counterpoint, the science of fugal stretto amongst other things. So let us now close this formal analysis with our second diagram summarizing all that has been said up to this point.

But before doing so, let us merely assert again that this study has had absolutly nothing to do with interpretation, symbolism, or theology. We have tried assiduously to look at the form simply as a mechanism and to examine it as coldly and objectively as possible. If, in a few instances, some interpretative implications have "overflowed," it is merely an indication that a pregnant artistic form cannot always—even with the most conscientious labor—be contained within its mechanical confines. So with this last word we leave the form to the reader for him to interpret and complete spiritually and artistically much as one must do in the case of an Oriental painting.

PART THE SECOND

About a fable by Aesop

CHAPTER XIV

What would you be doing if you were in jail for a month awaiting execution?

When Socrates found himself in this most unpleasant of predicaments the first thing he did was to write a hymn to Apollo, and then to rewrite Aesop's fables in poetic form.

We are given something of the background for this seemingly curious death-cell activity in the Phaedo of Plato. Socrates told his visitor Cebes that he had had for many years a recurring dream wherein he was always told the same thing, "Socrates, make music and work at it." Before going to prison he believed that this was exactly what he was doing, because to him "philosophy was the greatest kind of music," and he was most certainly "working at it."

But, after his trial he thought more about his dream and decided that it was a command to write poetry, and in so doing "to make this which is ordinarily called music." Whereupon Socrates, being by his own admission "not a maker of myths," took the fables of Aesop and turned them into verse.

To most students of the arts in our day no task could look more fruitless and less rewarding as preparation for the life beyond than the one Socrates undertook for himself. And yet, such a great thinker would surely not fritter away his last days on earth. Thus, it was decided not to put our observations on Dynamic Symmetry away until we had examined in some detail a fable by Aesop.

These fables are models of simplicity. But simplicity, as was said before, is the result of well-ordered complexity. And the greater the degree of complexity, the more pure and disarming is the simplicity. Many examples could be cited, but we shall content ourselves with one or two.

Once a class in harmony has learned about the basic triads and possibly the Dominant Seventh, it is rather customary to assign them a model composition—such as a minuet by Haydn—and after analyzing it, to require the students to use essentially the same chords and go on to compose a piece similar to the model. It all looks so easy. The chords are essentially those of the Tonic and the Dominant, and the form and cadences are all so straightforward and clean-cut.

But, what a disappointment when the student's composition is played! It sounds incredibly unlike the Haydn model, and yet it "looks" for all intents and purposes much the same. Some important ingredient of Haydn's music is missing, but what?

Simplicity, or more accurately "oneness," as the end result of complexity can be seen in another way. In monophonic music, such as in the Bach sonatas for unaccompanied violin, the single-line music embodies a complete texture of implied counterpoint. This contrapuntal background can be in as many parts as the composer's design and skill will permit, but it will be seen that as this background texture increases in intensity, the listener will be proportionately less aware of the several implied parts as these will have a tendency to merge into one single and indivisible line. However, in a simpler monophonic structure of only two implied parts as is often found in the sonatas of Handel and Corelli, these will always be heard quite separately and will never really merge into a single and indivisible line. In a different way this is true of a Harris tweed. When examined in detail the design of the weaving proves to be of incredible complexity, yet the over-all "effect" is extremely simple and plain.

Nowhere, however, do we find such complex simplicity as in the beloved fables of the Greek slave Aesop, who is said to have lived between 620 and 560 B. C.—roughly 2500 years ago. Most of these little fables, barely a page long, are at first glance merely miniature stories for children about animals, with a rather obvious moral. And, one might well ask, what is the infectious quality of them that has made them to endure for so long? Moreover, what about them is so important that Socrates devoted a good part of the last month of his life to transcribing them into poetic form?

We shall devote our remaining pages to an examination of one of these fables. We shall see how in a brief two-paragraph fable there is a veritable network of ideas and motives closely akin in their nature to a complicated fugue where subjects and countersubjects cavort about in double and triple counterpoint. And, one is tempted to ask whether this very complexity—so complex that it results in the most disarming simplicity—may not be the element that makes both a Bach fugue and an Aesop fable survive from century to century.

CHAPTER XV

Any discussion of the fables by Aesop presents the same problem that is present when one sets out to show how Bach's 371 Chorales are harmonized. Each one of the 2,265 lines contained in this collection of chorales is a veritable wonder of formal and harmonic planning, but no two are alike. So, what is to be done? It would be too much to go through every line, and if we examine only one or two as representative models, the student may get the impression that the scope of this technique is much narrower than it actually is.

However, being cognizant of this hazard and having stated it quite frankly to the reader, we have decided to examine the little tale about two mutually helpful friends, the Ant and the Dove and how they save each others' lives and outsmart a hunter. The fable fills scarcely more than half a page, and consists of two paragraphs the first of which is considerably longer than the second—the first visible sign of a Dynamic Symmetry structure.

THE ANT AND THE DOVE

A thirsty ant went to a spring for a drink of water. While climbing down a blade of grass to reach the spring he fell in. The ant might very well have drowned had it not been for a dove who happened to be perched on a near-by tree. Seeing the ant's danger the dove quickly plucked off a leaf and let it drop into the water near the struggling insect. The ant climbed upon the leaf and presently was wafted safely ashore.

Just at that time a hunter was spreading his net in the hope of snaring the dove. The gratified ant, perceiving the hunter's plan, bit him in the heel. Startled, the huntsman dropped his net, and the dove flew away to safety.

The matter of the two unequal paragraphs—a "rough and ready" demonstration of Dynamic Symmetry—has an interesting parallel. As has already been mentioned, Dr. Glenn Clark, in his *God's Reach*, points out that Jesus liked to give his parables in pairs, one being both longer and more intense than the other. The same inequality of sections exists in most instances of the so-called Two-Part Song Form in music which is, incidentally, one of the most difficult of musical forms to bring to a satisfactory conclusion. Likewise, in the familiar musical pair of Prelude and Fugue—which may or may not be joined by an "attacca"—there is invariably a difference both in dimension and intensity.

However this cursory view of the little fable about the mutually friendly Ant and Dove—in themselves quite unequal in size and function—leads us to the next level of examination, at which point we discover that in the number of sentences one of the most familiar Dynamic Symmetry ratios is in operation. The first paragraph contains *five* sentences and the second only *three:*

THE ANT AND THE DOVE

1. A thirsty ant went to a spring for a drink of water.
2. While climbing down a blade of grass to reach the spring he fell in.
3. The ant might very well have drowned had it not been for a dove who happened to be perched on a near-by tree.
4. Seeing the ant's danger the dove quickly plucked off a leaf and let it drop into the water near the struggling insect.
5. The ant climbed upon the leaf and presently was wafted safely ashore.

---

6. Just at that time a hunter was spreading his net in the hope of snaring the dove.
7. The gratified ant, perceiving the hunter's plan, bit him in the heel.
8. Startled, the huntsman dropped his net, and the dove flew away to safety.

111

It is to be noted that the endings of the two paragraphs have a striking similarity. The first and *larger* paragraph closes with the happy assurance that the *smaller* of the two characters, the Ant, "was wafted safely ashore." At the end of the second and *smaller* paragraph we read with delight that the *larger* of our two little friends, the Dove, "flew away to safety."

As said in an earlier chapter the 5:3 ratio is an important one. Most occidental rhythms and such commonplace musical forms as the eight-measure period as shown in Chapter VIII, are derived almost entirely from some application of this combination. But, many examples are not quite so obviously set forth as in the case in this fable.

Earlier it was demonstrated how in *A General Confession* as found in *The Book of Common Prayer*, the congregation confesses to five shortcomings and asks for three divine favors in return. This is usually printed in one paragraph, and this form is further concealed by the fact that this five plus three form is couched between introductory and "codetta" lines.

How this sort of order, as it comes into being through Dynamic Symmetry, permeates our environment through the most seemingly unrelated things is shown by the arrangement of vowels and consonants in our alphabet. With all of the foregoing observations as background, we merely subjoin a diagram of the alphabet with no additional comment except to mention that similar—though not identical—arrangements exist in both the Greek and Hebrew alphabets.

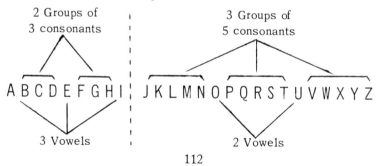

Superimposed upon the above plan near the end of it is a miniature form corresponding to the divisions at the beginning.

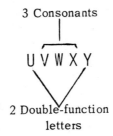

3 Consonants

U V W X Y

2 Double-function
letters

What a plan for systematizing the order of variations in a Passacaglia! And, what a pleasant discovery it is to find such impeccable order in so many commonplace things in one's everyday environment!

Parenthetically, it can be noted that on one occasion Jesus described himself in terms of the terminal letters of the Greek alphabet.

CHAPTER XVI

In the preceding chapter we penetrated the form of Aesop's fable about the Ant and the Dove through the visibly obvious arrangement of two unequal paragraphs to the second layer of organization; namely, the number of sentences within these two paragraphs.

Also, it was noted in passing that the three characters in the plot of this little fable in themselves demonstrate the simple $1:2$ ratio in several different ways. First, we meet up with *two* members of the animal world who are forced to match wits with *one* man. Secondly, we find these *two* little members of the animal world mutually helpful while the *one* man is their enemy. Finally, we find that *two* of our characters, the ant and the man, have to stay on the ground while *one* character, the dove, can fly.

As we study the fable more thoroughly it is seen that our *three* living characters—the ant, the dove and the hunter—carry out their little drama against a background of *five* inanimate objects:

a spring,
a blade of grass,
a leaf,
a tree,
a net.

As the story progresses each of the *three* living characters becomes associated with certain ones of the *five* inanimate objects, and here a most ingenious balance takes place. The ant, the *smallest* of the trio, becomes associated with *three* objects: the spring, the blade of grass and the leaf. The dove, the *second in size*, becomes associated with *two* objects: the tree and the leaf; while the hunter, by far the *largest* of the group, is associated with only *one* object: his net.

From here on the form is woven by means of sentence structure in a way that closely resembles a contrapuntal composition of such involved complexity that even Sergei Ivanovich Taneiev might not have thought of it in his most inventive moments. Before going into this in detail it might clarify the procedure if we write out the fable again in columnar form, but this time itemizing separately each element within the sentence since each one of these elements by means of a well-placed "part of speech" contains a complete picture of a condition, act or situation.

I. 1. (1) A thirsty *ant*
    (2) went to a *spring*
    (3) for a drink of water.
  2. (4) While climbing down a *blade of grass*
    (5) to reach the *spring*
    (6) he fell in.
  3. (7) The *ant* might very well have drowned
    (8) had it not been for a *dove*
    (9) who happened to be perched
    (10) in a nearby *tree*.
  4. (11) Seeing the *ant's* danger
    (12) the *dove* quickly plucked off a *leaf*
    (13) and let it drop into the water
    (14) near the struggling insect.
  5. (15) The *ant* climbed upon the *leaf*
    (16) and presently was wafted safely ashore.

II. 6. (17) Just at that time
    (18) a *hunter* was spreading his *net*
    (19) in the hope of snaring the *dove*.
  7. (20) The gratified *ant*,
    (21) perceiving the *hunter's* plan,
    (22) bit him in the heel.
  8. (23) Startled,
    (24) the *huntsman* dropped his *net*
    (25) and the *dove* flew away
    (26) to safety.

Here a whole network of Dynamic Symmetry ratios seem to spring into action. The over-all form of twenty-six sentence elements is divided by means of the two paragraphs into 16 + 10; the familiar ratio of 8:5 doubled.

Within the first paragraph many interesting things happen. The first *two* sentences deal solely with the ant and his misfortune. The remaining group of *three* sentences in this paragraph tell about the dove and its assistance to the ant. Thus, at first glance it looks as though the littlest of our friends, the ant, was given *two* sentences and the dove, many times the ant's size, was allotted *three* sentences. But wait!

If we look more closely we see that the first, second and fifth sentences are allotted to the ant alone; and actually only the third and fourth sentences concern the dove. So, here is a 3:2 ratio in favor of the ant.

However, it will be observed that in the matter of sentence elements the first *two* sentences contain six elements while the remaining three sentences of the first paragraph contain ten elements. Hence, the 2:3 ratio of sentences embody a 3:5 (i.e. 6 + 10) arrangement of sentence elements.

But, within the first paragraph these ratios also appear in retrograde. The dove, who appears in the third sentence, actually goes into action in the fourth sentence; thereby setting in motion the 3:2 ratio in the number of sentences *before* the dove acts to save the ant and the number of sentences *from* the action on. And the 5:3 ratio is maintained within the paragraph in that the first *three* sentences contain ten elements and the remaining *two* comprise six elements.

At this juncture we come upon a "joker." In spite of all this, the ant and the dove divide the sixteen sentence elements in this paragraph equally. In the three sentences given over exclusively to the ant, that is the first, second and fifth, there are eight elements; and in the third and fourth sentences in which the dove sees his little friend's danger and performs his heroic deed, there are likewise eight elements. Thus, upon finding that amongst so many complex ratios this paragraph is "halved" in an incredibly ingenious manner we may wish

116

to rethink the observations in an earlier chapter that discussed this division principle.

Turning again to the number of sentences, it is now clear that the *five* sentences in the first paragraph in which the dove befriends the hapless ant are balanced by *three* sentences of the second paragraph in which the hunter appears and is ultimately defeated in his attempt to capture the dove.

But, in the second paragraph, too, there is a subdivision into elements. There are six elements in the first *two* sentences that tell about the hunter's plan and the ant's cleverness and four elements in the remaining *one* sentence that tells about the hunter's defeat and the dove's escape.

The counterpoint of ideas can be shown very simply in a diagram. To add significance visually we will consider the three living characters as Subjects I, II and III (as in a triple fugue) and the inanimate objects as Countersubjects I, II, III, IV and V, or subordinate or complementary thematic material. From this angle the form appears thus:

I.

1.   2.

Ant (Sub. I)

Spring (C. S. I)   Spring (C. S. I)

                 Blade of grass (C. S. II)

3.   4.   5.

Ant (Sub. I)   Ant (Sub. I)   Ant (Sub. I)

Dove (Sub. II)   Dove (Sub. II)

Tree (C. S. III) Leaf (C. S. IV) Leaf (C. S. IV)

II.

6.   7.   8.

Hunter (Sub. III) Ant (Sub. I)   Hunter (Sub. III)

Dove (Sub. II)   Hunter (Sub. III) Dove (Sub. II)

Net (C. S. V)   Net (C. S. V)

What a scheme for a polyphonic composition!

More need not be said about the fable. The foregoing may provide some hints as to the importance of Aesop's forms and at least one probable reason why Socrates spent his last month putting these into poetic form. Are we being presumptious to ask in closing whether form: the silent language might not have spoken with unusual clarity to Socrates?

Before putting this little book away, let us reread the fable in a relaxed spirit and enjoy the delightful and restful simplicity it achieves through so much complexity.

A thirsty ant went to a spring for a drink of water. While climbing down a blade of grass to reach the spring he fell in. The ant might very well have drowned had it not been for a dove who happened to be perched on a near-by tree. Seeing the ant's danger the dove quickly plucked off a leaf and let it drop into the water near the struggling insect. The ant climbed upon the leaf and presently was wafted safely ashore.

Just at that time a hunter was spreading his net in the hope of snaring the dove. The gratified ant, perceiving the hunter's plan, bit him in the heel. Startled, the huntsman dropped his net, and the dove flew away to safety.

Application: One good turn deserves another.

EPILOGUE

After having touched upon so many things the reader may feel as though he had been in contact with the genial walrus who had decided that the time had come to talk of many things, "of shoes and ships and sealing-wax, and cabbages and kings." But, that is one of the effects of Dynamic Symmetry: it brings together all good and beautiful things.

Some readers may be fearful of Dynamic Symmetry, and consider it to be a rigid and artificial technique upon which unimaginative and artistically sterile craftsmen may lean in their futile attempts at creativity. But this is not at all the case. Those who are skilled in Dynamic Symmetry—and skill in this field is really only a high degree of awareness—find in it a force that not only releases their creativity, but transforms it. Or, to word it more simply, Dynamic Symmetry leads one to do much better what he would do quite naturally. It dispels artificiality and ineptness.

But, more than this, Dynamic Symmetry does something else for everybody: it eliminates once and for all time any trace of boredom. Everything, no matter how commonplace, becomes alive and interesting and full of structural wonders. And, thus, we see significance in the quotation from Walt Whitman with which our Prologue began, and being cognizant of its implications, we take the liberty to close with an amplification of it by the same gifted American poet:

Beginning my studies the first step pleas'd me so much,
The mere fact consciousness, these forms, the power of motion,
The least insect or animal, the senses, eyesight, love,
The first step I say awed me and pleas'd me so much,
I have hardly gone and hardly wish'd to go any farther,
But stop and loiter all the time to sing it in ecstatic songs.

That just about sums up the whole purpose of this book. And, in quite different terms and in a contrasting spirit, an old Jewish Doxology puts it this way—

Formless, all lovely forms
Declare his loveliness.

119

INDEX

121